Acts: model for today's church

Bible Study That Builds Christian Community

SERENDIPITY
H O U S E

LIFE
CONNECTIONS

To order additional copies of this resource:
ORDER ONLINE at *www.serendipityhouse.com*;
VISIT the LifeWay Christian Store serving you;
WRITE Serendipity House
117 10th Avenue, North
Nashville, TN 37234
FAX (615) 277-8181
PHONE (800) 525-9563

Printed in the United States of America

117 10th Avenue, North
Nashville, Tennessee 37234

Contents

Core Values

Community: The purpose of this curriculum is to build community within the body of believers around Jesus Christ.

Group Process: To build community, the curriculum must be designed to take a group through a step-by-step process of sharing your story with one another.

Interactive Bible Study: To share your "story," the approach to Scripture in the curriculum needs to be open-ended and right-brained—to "level the playing field" and encourage everyone to share.

Developmental Stages: To provide a healthy program in the life cycle of a group, the curriculum needs to offer courses on three levels of commitment:

(1) Beginner Level—low-level entry, high structure, to level the playing field;
(2) Growth Level—deeper Bible study, flexible structure, to encourage group accountability;
(3) Discipleship Level—in-depth Bible study, open structure, to move the group into high gear.

Target Audiences: To build community throughout the culture of the church, the curriculum needs to be flexible, adaptable, and transferable into the structure of the average church.

Mission: To expand the kingdom of God one person at a time by filling the "empty chair." (We add an extra chair to each group session to remind us of our mission.)

Group Covenant

It is important that your group covenant together, agreeing to live out important group values. Once these values are agreed upon, your group will be on its way to experiencing Christian community. It's very important that your group discuss these values—preferably as you begin this study. The first session would be most appropriate. (Check the rules to which each member of your group agrees.)

☐ **Priority:** While you are in this course of study, you give the group meetings priority.

☐ **Participation:** Everyone is encouraged to participate and no one dominates.

☐ **Respect:** Everyone is given the right to his or her own opinion, and all questions are encouraged and respected.

☐ **Confidentiality:** Anything that is said in the meeting is never repeated outside the meeting.

☐ **Life Change:** We will regularly assess our own life-change goals and encourage one another in our pursuit of Christlikeness.

☐ **Empty Chair:** The group stays open to reaching new people at every meeting.

☐ **Care and Support:** Permission is given to call upon each other at any time, especially in times of crisis. The group will provide care for every member.

☐ **Accountability:** We agree to let the members of the group hold us accountable to the commitments we make in whatever loving ways we decide upon.

☐ **Mission:** We will do everything in our power to start a new group.

☐ **Ministry:** The group will encourage one another to volunteer and serve in a ministry and to support missions by giving financially and/or personally serving.

notes

Called to Action

Prepare for the Session

	READINGS	REFLECTIVE QUESTIONS
Monday	Acts 1:1–3	What has Christ done to show you that He is alive?
Tuesday	Acts 1:4–8	Where is Christ calling you to witness this week?
Wednesday	Acts 1:9	What "cloud" sometimes hides Christ from you? How can you dispel this "cloud"?
Thursday	Acts 1:10–11	What are you doing to make sure you are prepared when Christ returns?
Friday	Acts 1:14	How well are you disciplining yourself in prayer? Is your prayer life "hit-and-miss" or are you going to God regularly?
Saturday	Acts 1:15–17	When has one you considered a Christian friend failed you? How well are you dealing with that failure?
Sunday	Acts 1:24	What is God, who knows your heart, calling you to do with your life right now?

BIBLE STUDY

- to consider Jesus' last words to His disciples and how His words apply to our mission
- to better understand what we are called to do in relationship to what God is doing in the world
- to begin looking at the role of the Holy Spirit in empowering the church to action

LIFE CHANGE

- to adopt a missionary
- to visit a local ministry in our hometown
- to spend some time in conversation with a non-Christian acquaintance or loved one

Icebreaker

10-15 minutes

**GATHERING
THE PEOPLE
ⵙ Form
horseshoe
groups of 6–8.**

Saying Good-byes. Go around the group on question 1 and let everyone share. Then go around again on question 2.

1. In which of the following life situations did you have the hardest time saying good-bye? Mark your answer with an "H." In which of these situations did you have the easiest time? Mark your answer with an "E."

___ when I first went to kindergarten

___ when I got married or left home to go to college

___ when I graduated from high school and had to say good-bye to friends

___ when I left my first job

___ when a pastor at my church left for another position

___ when my first child went to kindergarten

___ when my child got married or left home to go to college

2. When it comes to saying good-bye, which of the following approaches do you most often use?

☐ I drag out all the hugs and tears for as long as I can.

☐ I make it quick and painless.

☐ I just leave and don't say anything.

Bible Study

30-45 minutes

The Scripture for this week:

¹*In my former book, Theophilus, I wrote about all that Jesus began to do and to teach* ²*until the day he was taken up to heaven, after giving instructions through the Holy Spirit to the apostles he had chosen.* ³*After his suffering, he showed himself to these men and gave many convincing proofs that he was alive. He appeared to them over a period of forty days and spoke about the kingdom of God.* ⁴*On one occasion, while he was eating with them, he gave them this command: "Do not leave Jerusalem, but wait for the gift my Father promised, which you have heard me speak about.* ⁵*For John baptized with water, but in a few days you will be baptized with the Holy Spirit."*

⁶*So when they met together, they asked him, "Lord, are you at this time going to restore the kingdom to Israel?"*

⁷*He said to them: "It is not for you to know the times or dates the Father has set by his own authority.* ⁸*But you will receive power when the Holy Spirit comes on you; and you will be my witnesses in Jerusalem, and in all Judea and Samaria, and to the ends of the earth."*

⁹*After he said this, he was taken up before their very eyes, and a cloud hid him from their sight.*

¹⁰*They were looking intently up into the sky as he was going, when suddenly two men dressed in white stood beside them.* ¹¹*"Men of Galilee," they said, "why do you stand here looking into the sky? This same Jesus, who has been taken from you into heaven, will come back in the same way you have seen him go into heaven."*

...about today's session

A WORD
FROM THE
LEADER

Write your
answers
here.

1. What are people who fail to learn from church history doomed to do? *not to repeat it*

2. What should a church do when the members feel they are not doing any kind of mighty work for the Lord?

They need to look at acts and remember Holy Spirit is their source of power

Identifying with the Story

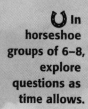 **In horseshoe groups of 6–8, explore questions as time allows.**

1. When you were an adolescent or younger adult, who did you consider to be your mentor? In what area of life did you learn the most from this person?

2. How would you describe your mentoring status right now in terms of this story?

   ☐ I'm still receiving mentoring, like the apostles did during the 40 days.

   ☐ I'm desiring mentoring, like the apostles did after Jesus ascended.

   ☐ I'm ready to act on my own, like the disciples did later at Pentecost.

   ☐ I'm ready to mentor others, like Luke did through the writing of Acts.

   ☐ I'm not sure that I would be comfortable either mentoring or being mentored.

3. Had you been with Jesus when He was getting ready to return to heaven, what one last question would you have asked Him?

today's session

What is God teaching you from this story?

1. Three different ways of looking at the human role and responsibility for changing the world are:
   God is not going to do anything, so we
   a. _have to do everything_
   God will do everything, so we
   b. _don't have to do anything_
   God will act and an important part of
   c. _his action will be what he does through_

2. The Book of Acts is the story of how Jesus began to fulfill what promise? _that his_
   Disciples will be able to do even
   greater things he has done - if they
   act in his name

10

3. Why did Jesus want the disciples to wait for the gift of the Holy Spirit? *God was telling them to wait until God empowered them to act*

4. How did Jesus seek to expand the disciples' view of what their mission was? *Told them to start in Ieruslem and go to the ends of the earth*

5. What parable of Jesus is cited to illustrate what we should be doing while waiting for Christ to return?
Sevant who is doing his job when the master returns.

Learning from the Story

In horseshoe groups of 6–8, choose an answer and explain why you chose what you did.

1. What "convincing proofs" (v. 3) have you seen that Jesus Christ really is alive?

2. In verse 8, Jesus says "you will be my witnesses." Where do you feel most called to witness for Christ?

   ☐ to my family members
   ☐ to my co-workers
   ☐ to people in my neighborhood
   ☐ to people in the "Third World"
   ☐ none of the above—The whole idea of witnessing scares me to death!
   ☐ other: _____

3. How much power do you feel you are getting from the Holy Spirit right now?

   ☐ not enough to keep a smoke detector from "chirping"
   ☐ maybe enough to put a weak beam on a flashlight, but that's about it
   ☐ enough to run a child's toy—The Energizer Bunny would be proud!
   ☐ enough to run a major home appliance
   ☐ enough to supply the energy needs for a small city

life change lessons

1. In what two ways can the vision of your mission get out of balance?

   a. _____

   b. _____

2. Where can you find a list of missionaries with whom you might correspond?

Caring Time

15-20 minutes

CARING TIME

◡ Remain in horseshoe groups of 6–8.

This is the time to develop and express your care for each other. Begin by having each group member finish the sentence:

> *"The area of my life where I really need the guidance of the Holy Spirit is ..."*

Pray for these concerns and any others that are listed on the Prayer/Praise Report. Include prayer for the empty chair.

If you would like to pray silently, say "Amen" when you have finished your prayer, so that the next person will know when to start.

Reference Notes

BIBLE STUDY NOTES

Use these notes to gain further understanding of the text as you study on your own.

ACTS 1:1

my former book. That is, the Gospel of Luke. Church tradition is unanimous in its witness that Luke authored both works.
Theophilus. An unknown figure.
all that Jesus began to do and to teach. This is a clue to the way one should view this book—it is the continuing story of the work of Jesus through His Spirit in the life of His body, the church.

ACTS 1:2

until the day he was taken up to heaven. See Luke 24:50-53. The ascension does not mark the end of Jesus' ministry, but simply a new

ACTS 1:2 (cont'd) phase of His work. He now exercises his divine reign from heaven.

through the Holy Spirit. The Spirit played an important part in the earthly ministry of Jesus (in His conception—Luke 1:35; in His presentation—Luke 2:25-28; as a summary of His purpose—Luke 3:16; in His baptism—Luke 3:22; in His temptation—Luke 4:1; in His teaching—Luke 4:14; in His prayer; and in His expectations for the future—Luke 24:49).

apostles. See Luke 6:12-16. Apostles were ambassadors especially commissioned to represent the one in whose name they were sent.

ACTS 1:3 In the Gospel, Luke went to some length to underscore the reality of the physical resurrection of Jesus so that his readers could be assured the apostles were not seeing a ghost (Luke 24:37-42). However, he did not mention the span of time over which the appearances occurred. Matthew and John record a couple of these later appearances prior to the ascension.

the kingdom of God. The announcement of the reign of God through which He saves His people was the theme of Jesus' earthly ministry as well (Luke 4:43).

ACTS 1:4–5 ***the gift my Father promised.*** This gift is the Holy Spirit. (See Isa. 32:15; Joel 2:28-32; Luke 11:13; 12:12; 24:49; Gal. 3:14.) Jesus quotes the words of John the Baptist (Luke 3:16) as a reminder that from the very beginning the expectation was that through Him the Spirit of God would be poured out on all His people.

baptized with the Holy Spirit. Baptism was associated with cleansing. The metaphor would communicate a being flooded with God's Spirit. Thus, Jesus raised the expectations of the disciples regarding what the next step in His agenda for them might be.

ACTS 1:8 This verse embraces the twin themes of the whole book. The mission of Jesus is continued through the work of His Spirit empowering and enabling the disciples to bear witness to Him (Matt. 28:19-20; Luke 12:11-12). The result of this empowering will be the spread of the gospel throughout the world—from the spiritual heart of Israel (Jerusalem), to the immediate vicinity (Judea), to the despised Samaritans in the adjacent province to the north, to the outermost reaches of the earth. The book of Acts is built around these geographical markers. Chapters 1:1–6:7 occur in Jerusalem and Judea; 6:8–8:40 deals with events that lead the church to Samaria; and 9:1 on recounts the chain of events that leads Paul to journey throughout much of the Roman Empire with the good news of Jesus.

ACTS 1:9 ***a cloud hid him from their sight.*** This is not a statement of weather conditions at the time, but a declaration of Jesus' deity. See also Daniel 7:13-14.

ACTS 1:11 The Mount of Olives, where the ascension occurred (v. 12), was just outside of the city. The angels' message picks up on Zechariah 14:4, which teaches that the Messiah will one day appear on a mountain when He comes to fully establish His reign.

notes

Power from Above

Prepare for the Session

	READINGS	REFLECTIVE QUESTIONS
Monday	Acts 2:1–4	How has the Holy Spirit been at work in your life?
Tuesday	Acts 2:5–13	What has God done recently that amazed you?
Wednesday	Acts 2:22–23	How would you like to thank God for what He did for you through the death of His Son Jesus Christ?
Thursday	Acts 2:29–32	Consider how Christ's victory over death has affected your own feelings about your mortality. Does fear of death keep you from fully living your life?
Friday	Acts 2:36–38	Because of what Christ has done for you, what should you be doing for Him?
Saturday	Acts 2:39	Consider how well are you conveying the good news of Jesus Christ to the next generation—to your own children or to nephews, nieces, or children in your sphere of influence?
Sunday	Acts 2:40–41	What might God be warning you about right now in your life? How responsive are you to warnings?

BIBLE STUDY
- to gain a better understanding of what happened when the Holy Spirit came at Pentecost
- to appreciate the power of the Spirit to bring diverse peoples together
- to consider how the Holy Spirit empowers the church today

LIFE CHANGE
- to pray for the Holy Spirit's presence and power
- to commit one day to following the Holy Spirit's guidance
- to encourage our church in one new venture of faith

Icebreaker

10-15 minutes

Fired Up. Check which of each of the following pairs is most likely to get you "fired up."

a powerful sermon · a powerful song

rock music · a marching band

an appeal to my
compassionate side ·

an appeal to my
competitive side

a story of injustice · a story of romance

praise hymns · a dramatic, traditional hymn

Information to Remember: In the spaces provided, take note of information you will need as you participate in this group in the weeks to come.

PEOPLE:

1. The person in this group who has the biggest smile today is:

2. The person in the group who looks like they could use a hug is:

EVENTS: An event that is coming up that I want to make sure I am part of is _____. It will be _____ (time) on _____ (date) at _____ (location).

And if I have time, I would also like to be part of _____. It will be _____ (time) on _____ (date) at _____ (location).

Bible Study

30-45 minutes

The Scripture for this week:

[1]*When the day of Pentecost came, they were all together in one place.* [2]*Suddenly a sound like the blowing of a violent wind came from heaven and filled the whole house where they were sitting.* [3]*They saw what seemed to be tongues of fire that separated and came to rest on each of them.* [4]*All of them were filled with the Holy Spirit and began to speak in other tongues as the Spirit enabled them.*

[5]*Now there were staying in Jerusalem God-fearing Jews from every nation under heaven.* [6]*When they heard this sound, a crowd came together in bewilderment, because each one heard them speaking in his own language.* [7]*Utterly amazed, they asked: "Are not all these men who are speaking Galileans?* [8]*Then how is it that each of us hears them in his own native language?* [9]*Parthians, Medes and Elamites; residents of Mesopotamia, Judea and Cappadocia, Pontus and Asia,* [10]*Phrygia and Pamphylia, Egypt and the parts of Libya near Cyrene; visitors from Rome* [11]*(both Jews and converts to Judaism); Cretans and Arabs—we hear them declaring the wonders of God in our own tongues!"* [12]*Amazed and perplexed, they asked one another, "What does this mean?"*

[13]*Some, however, made fun of them and said, "They have had too much wine."*

...about today's session

A WORD
FROM THE
LEADER

Write your
answers
here.

1. What question do we need to ask of the church if it is not "working" properly?

2. What promise is God fulfilling in our passage for today?

Identifying with the Story

U In
horseshoe
groups of 6–8,
explore
questions as
time allows.

1. When have you had an experience in a group that was so amazing and unique you had a hard time explaining it to people who weren't there?

   ☐ at a camp or a conference
   ☐ at a concert
   ☐ at a sporting event
   ☐ on a trip
   ☐ at a very special worship service
   ☐ other: _____

2. With what other cultures have you had contact? Were the relationships between the cultures in your neighborhood or town relaxed or tense?

3. What adult do you remember who really "spoke your language" when you were an adolescent?

today's session

What is God
teaching you
from this
story?

1. What was the importance of Pentecost before it became the birthday of the church?

2. What three different English words translate the Hebrew word *rhuah* and the Greek word *pneuma*?

    a. _____

    b. _____

    c. _____

3. What phrases does the Old Testament use to refer to the Holy Spirit?

4. What two uncontrollable forces are used to represent the Holy Spirit in this passage?

    a. _____

    b. _____

5. The church must _____ the power of the Holy Spirit.

6. The events of this passage are a reverse of what Old Testament story?

7. God can only do great things through us if we _____ _____ _____ for God.

Learning from the Story

In horseshoe groups of 6–8, choose an answer and explain why you chose what you did.

1. Had you been present when the Holy Spirit came upon the disciples at Pentecost, who would you have been more like—those who were amazed by the wonders of God, or those who thought the disciples were drunk? Mark where you would be on the scale below.

1 · · · · · · · · · 2 · · · · · · · · · 3 · · · · · · · · · · 4 · · · · · · · · · 5

those who
were amazed

those who
thought
them drunk

2. What do you feel you most need the power of the Holy Spirit to do in your life right now?

☐ to help me connect with others, as when the "cultural gap" was bridged at Pentecost

☐ to help me learn more of "the wonders of God"

☐ to help me be used to share "the wonders of God"

☐ other: _____

3. If you were to share just one "wonder of God" that you have experienced, what would it be?

life change lessons

1. What two things must we not do in relation to this study?

a. _____

b. _____

2. What difference do some people see between the church of today and the church of Peter and Paul? How accurate is that perception?

Caring Time

15-20 minutes

During this prayer time, thank God for the "wonders of God" that group members have experienced in their lives. Take turns praying for each other, asking for the Holy Spirit's presence and power to fill each person's life and ministry. Also, use the Prayer/Praise Report and pray for the concerns listed.

Close by praying specifically for God to guide you to someone to invite for next week to fill the empty chair.

Reference Notes

**BIBLE
STUDY
NOTES**

Use these notes to gain further understanding
of the text as you study on your own.

**ACTS
2:1**

the day of Pentecost. This was the Feast of Weeks (Ex. 23:16; Lev. 23:15-21; Deut. 16:9-12) held fifty days after Passover. Originally a kind of Thanksgiving Day for gathered crops, it came to be associated with the commemoration of the giving of the Law at Sinai (Ex. 20:1-17). Jewish tradition held that when God gave the Law to Moses, a single voice spoke that was heard by all the nations of the world in their own language. Luke may be alluding to that in this story. Pentecost was a celebration which thousands of Jews from all over the empire would attend.

2

**ACTS
2:2–4**

The Greek word for "wind" and "spirit" is the same, hence the symbolism of the Spirit coming like a great wind. Fire is often associated with divine appearances (Ex. 3:2; 19:18). John the Baptist said Jesus would baptize His followers with the Holy Spirit and fire (Luke 3:16), symbolizing the cleansing, purifying effect of the Spirit. What is important here is that tongues served as a sign to the crowds of a supernatural event, the point of which was Jesus Christ.

**ACTS
2:4**

filled with the Holy Spirit. This phrase is found elsewhere (Acts 4:8,31; 13:52; Eph. 5:18) indicating a repeatable experience. Here, however, it is clearly associated with the baptism of the Spirit (Acts 1:5), which is an experience new converts enter into upon acceptance of Jesus as the Messiah (Acts 2:41).

**ACTS
2:5–8**

The disciples apparently made their way to the temple where they attracted a large crowd that was puzzled over how they could speak in their native dialects.

**ACTS
2:9-11**

Parthians, Medes and Elamites ... Mesopotamia. Present-day Iran and Iraq, to the east of Jerusalem. These Jews traced their roots back to the Assyrian overthrow of Israel and the Babylonian overthrow of Judea seven and five centuries beforehand respectively.
Judea. Either the immediate environs around Jerusalem is in view, or Luke is thinking of the days under David and Solomon when the land of Israel stretched from Egypt on the west to the Euphrates River on the east.
Cappadocia, Pontus and Asia, Phrygia and Pamphylia. Present-day Turkey to the north of Jerusalem. Much of Acts takes place in this region.
Egypt ... Libya near Cyrene. To the west of Jerusalem on the northern coast of Africa.
converts to Judaism. Judaism's high morality and developed spirituality attracted many Gentiles in other religions.
Cretans. An island south of Greece in the Mediterranean Sea.
Arabs. The Nabetean kingdom was south of Jerusalem with borders on Egypt and the Euphrates.

21

notes

3

A New Kind of Community

Prepare for the Session

	READINGS	REFLECTIVE QUESTIONS
Monday	Acts 2:42–45	How are you ministering to the needs of the believers around you?
Tuesday	Acts 2:46–47	Can you honestly say that you have a glad heart at this point in your life? If not, why not?
Wednesday	Acts 3:2–7	What do you have that you can give others in the name of Jesus Christ? How generously are you giving this?
Thursday	Acts 3:9–10	How might people see you as being changed because of the way Christ has touched you?
Friday	Acts 3:16	What weaknesses do you have that need to be made strong by Jesus Christ? Are you trusting God to strengthen them?
Saturday	Acts 3:19–20	What is God calling you to repent of right now?
Sunday	Acts 4:1–20	Do you feel the same compulsion that Peter and John felt to share what Christ has done for you? If not, why not?

BIBLE STUDY

- to look at the nature of the community of the early church
- to determine what factors made the early church so effective
- to see how emulating certain qualities of the early church might make today's churches more powerful

LIFE CHANGE

- to find one new way we can minister to each other's needs
- to invite others over to our homes
- to work together on a group covenant

Icebreaker

10-15 minutes

It's Better Together. Go around the group on question 1 and let everyone share. Then go around on question 2.

1. Which of the following activities would you rather do with friends? Which would you prefer to do alone? Mark those you prefer to do with friends with an "F," and mark those you prefer to do alone with an "A."

___ eating lunch or dinner   ___ driving on a long trip
___ watching television   ___ shopping
___ going to a sporting event   ___ worshiping God
___ fishing

2. Pick one of the activities you said you prefer to do with friends. What is the most important quality you look for in someone with whom to do this activity?

☐ similar interests   ☐ nonjudgmental
☐ easy to talk to   ☐ someone I can be myself with
☐ good sense of humor   ☐ a good listener
☐ empathetic   ☐ strong moral values

Information to Remember: In the spaces provided, take note of information you will need as you participate in this group in the weeks to come.

PEOPLE:

1. A person in the group I might enjoy doing something with outside class is:

2. A person who is not here who might enjoy a phone call is:

EVENTS: An event that is coming up that I want to make sure I am part of is _____. It will be _____ (time) on _____ (date) at _____ (location).

And if I have time, I would also like to be part of _____. It will be _____ (time) on _____ (date) at _____ (location).

Bible Study
30-45 minutes

The Scripture for this week:

LEARNING FROM THE BIBLE

ACTS 2:42–47

⁴²They devoted themselves to the apostles' teaching and to the fellowship, to the breaking of bread and to prayer. ⁴³Everyone was filled with awe, and many wonders and miraculous signs were done by the apostles. ⁴⁴All the believers were together and had everything in common. ⁴⁵Selling their possessions and goods, they gave to anyone as he had need. ⁴⁶Every day they continued to meet together in the temple courts. They broke bread in their homes and ate together with glad and sincere hearts, ⁴⁷praising God and enjoying the favor of all the people. And the Lord added to their number daily those who were being saved.

...about today's session

A WORD FROM THE LEADER

Write your answers here.

1. What is one example of a product that might be developed from a prototype?

2. What does it mean to make the church of Acts a prototype for churches today?

Identifying with the Story

In horseshoe groups of 6–8, explore questions as time allows.

1. When have you experienced a fellowship like these believers had together?

   ☐ with a group of high school friends
   ☐ with a group of college friends
   ☐ at a conference where everyone got really close
   ☐ with a church small group
   ☐ never
   ☐ other: _____

2. Which of the factors present in this story is most important to you in developing fellowship with other believers? Rank them in order from "1" (most important) to "6" (least important):

   ___ devotion to common teaching and belief (v. 42)
   ___ praying together (v. 42)
   ___ doing exciting, wondrous works together (v. 43)
   ___ caring for each other's physical, emotional, and spiritual needs (vv. 44-45)
   ___ regular, common worship that includes praising God (vv. 46—7)
   ___ doing everyday things together, like eating and being in each other's homes (v. 46)

3. Which of the factors listed in question 2 is missing most in your present relationships with other believers?

today's session

What is God teaching you from this story?

1. How often were people saved in the church described in this passage?

2. What were some of the "wonders and miraculous signs" being done by the apostles?

3. What are some of the human needs to which today's church might respond?

4. What is one contributing factor to the social need experienced in our country?

5. Ministering to people's spiritual needs might mean bringing healing to what aspects of their lives?

6. What is the relationship between religious activity and health, according to a growing number of medical studies?

Learning from the Story

In horseshoe groups of 6–8, choose an answer and explain why you chose what you did.

1. How do you relate to the early church's practice of having "everything in common" (v. 44)?

   ☐ It is communistic!
   ☐ It is naive, though well-intentioned.
   ☐ It is the way things should be in the church.
   ☐ I can't see myself ever being part of such a practice.
   ☐ I think I could really get into a community that did this.

2. Which of the factors present in this story do you think most contributed to the result that "the Lord added to their number daily those who were being saved" (v. 47)?

   ☐ devotion to common teaching and belief (v. 42)
   ☐ praying together (v. 42)
   ☐ doing a lot of exciting, wondrous works together (v. 43)
   ☐ caring for each other's physical, emotional, and spiritual needs (vv. 44-45)
   ☐ regular, common worship that includes praising God (vv. 46-47)
   ☐ doing everyday things together, like eating and being in each other's homes (v. 46)

3. Were your church to minister to the greatest need of the people in your community, what need would that be, and what would your church need to "sell" or sacrifice to minister to that need?

life change lessons

1. How does the idea of "fellowship" as displayed in this passage of Acts compare to the idea of "fellowship" as many modern churches understand it?

2. What are some aspects of church life we need to look at in order to truly strengthen church fellowship?

Caring Time

15-20 minutes

Remember that this is the time for expressing your concern for each other as group members and for supporting one another in prayer. Begin by having each group member finish this sentence:

> *"The area of need where this group could minister to me this week is ..."*

Pray for these needs, in addition to the concerns listed on the Prayer/Praise Report. Remember to pray for God's guidance in inviting someone to the group next week to fill the empty chair.

Reference Notes

Use these notes to gain further understanding
of the text as you study on your own.

**ACTS
2:42**

The four components of the church's life listed here may represent what occurred at their gatherings.

teaching. The foundation for the church's life was the instruction given by the apostles as the representatives of Jesus.

fellowship. Literally, "sharing." While this may include the aspect of sharing to meet material needs (v. 45), it most likely means their common participation in the Spirit as they worshiped together (1 Cor. 12).

the breaking of bread. The Lord's Supper in which they remembered Jesus' death (Luke 22:19) and recognized His presence among them (Luke 24:30-31).

to prayer. Literally, "the prayers." This may refer to set times and forms of prayer as was the practice of the Jews.

**ACTS
2:43–47**

The picture of the church is one of continual growth (vv. 43,47), marked by generous sharing (vv. 44-45), and joyful worship and fellowship (vv. 46-47). The worship at the temple continued as before since the line dividing Christianity from Judaism had not yet been drawn. Christians simply saw their faith as the natural end of what the Jewish faith had always declared.

**ACTS
2:44–45**

everything in common. While this was a primitive form of socialism, it certainly did not include the oppressive totalitarianism or denial of God found in many modern forms. It was simply an outgrowth of the intense love people had for each other through Jesus Christ. They believed that in Christ each person's need becomes everyone's need.

**ACTS
2:47**

And the Lord added. Growth in the church was a natural result of the love, fellowship, and commitment to the apostle's teaching, which this section describes.

notes

When Conflict
Hits the Church

Prepare for the Session

4

	READINGS	REFLECTIVE QUESTIONS
Monday	Acts 6:1–7	What special ministry might God be calling you to do in your church or community?
Tuesday	Acts 7:37–43	Consider the false gods around you in the world. Which ones are you tempted to worship?
Wednesday	Acts 7:51–53	How are you stubbornly resisting God's Word for your life right now? What would help you be more open to that Word?
Thursday	Acts 7:57–60	How well are you doing forgiving those who have done harm to you?
Friday	Acts 8:1–8	How has God taken the bad things that have happened to you and used them for good?
Saturday	Acts 8:30–31	What spiritual issues are you having trouble understanding right now? Who might be able to help you with your struggle?
Sunday	Acts 8:36–40	What is the next step God is calling you toward in your Christian growth? How willing are you to take that step?

BIBLE STUDY

- to examine a conflict situation in the early church and see what we can learn from it
- to consider how tasks were delegated in the early church according to gifts
- to see how conflict is natural and unavoidable even in a church setting

LIFE CHANGE

- to visit with the pastor and several lay people to find out who are the disaffected groups in our church
- to compare the makeup of the governing board or body of our church with the makeup of the congregation as a whole
- to pray for people in our church who have a different perspective or need than us and the groups of which we feel a part

Icebreaker

10-15 minutes

Myself as an Appliance. In any well-functioning group, different people must take different roles. What is your role in your family? Go around the group on question 1 and let everyone share. Then go around on question 2.

1. If you could compare the role you have taken in your family to a household appliance, what appliance would it be?

- ☐ the vacuum cleaner—I pick up after everyone.
- ☐ the washing machine agitator—When things get too calm I stir things up.
- ☐ the heater—When people come in from the cold world I warm them up.
- ☐ the television—I'm the entertainer.
- ☐ the smoke alarm—I keep others alert to dangers.
- ☐ the thermostat—I keep things comfortable.
- ☐ the refrigerator—I provide all of the good stuff people seem to want.
- ☐ the electric screwdriver—I fix things and keep them running.

2. How happy are you with this role right now?

Information to Remember: Finish the following sentences as you look around at the people here today.

1. The person in the group today whom I know the least is:

2. Something I could do to get to know this person better is:

Bible Study
30-45 minutes

The Scripture for this week:

¹*In those days when the number of disciples was increasing, the Grecian Jews among them complained against the Hebraic Jews because their widows were being overlooked in the daily distribution of food.* ²*So the Twelve gathered all the disciples together and said, "It would not be right for us to neglect the ministry of the word of God in order to wait on tables.* ³*Brothers, choose seven men from among you who are known to be full of the Spirit and wisdom. We will turn this responsibility over to them* ⁴*and will give our attention to prayer and the ministry of the word."*

⁵*This proposal pleased the whole group. They chose Stephen, a man full of faith and of the Holy Spirit; also Philip, Procorus, Nicanor, Timon, Parmenas, and Nicolas from Antioch, a convert to Judaism.* ⁶*They presented these men to the apostles, who prayed and laid their hands on them.*

⁷*So the word of God spread. The number of disciples in Jerusalem increased rapidly, and a large number of priests became obedient to the faith.*

...about today's session

A WORD
FROM THE
LEADER

Write your
answers
here.

1. What examples of modern church conflicts are mentioned here? What examples could you add to the list?

2. Fill in the blank: "... though the church has a divine commission, it has a decidedly human membership; and where there are human beings, there will be _____." Do you agree with this statement? Why or why not?

Identifying with the Story

1. What are people in the household where you live most likely to complain about?

   ☐ nothing to eat in the house
   ☐ someone else having control of the TV remote
   ☐ other people's clutter
   ☐ someone else using the computer
   ☐ someone else monopolizing the phone
   ☐ lack of time spent together
   ☐ respect their personal space
   ☐ other: _____

2. Which of the following phrases best typifies your approach to dealing with complaints? Is there a difference between how you respond at work and at home?

   ☐ "Here's the world's smallest violin playing, 'My heart bleeds for you'!"
   ☐ "It's my way or the highway!"
   ☐ "You can't please all of the people all of the time."
   ☐ "You have a right to your opinion."
   ☐ "File a report and we'll talk."
   ☐ "It's probably my fault."
   ☐ "Anything to make you happy."

3. When have you felt like you were "being overlooked" (v. 1) in a church situation?

today's session

1. What were some of the differences between Grecian and Hebraic Jews?

4

2. Why was it especially important at this time to take care of the needs of widows?

3. What does Paul say in 1 Corinthians 13 is the greatest gift of all? How does this relate to those who used their gifts to "wait on tables"?

4. Why is it significant that those selected to these positions all had Greek names?

5. Why did the Twelve "lay their hands on" these new church leaders?

6. What eventually happened to Stephen?

Learning from the Story

In horseshoe groups of 6–8, choose an answer and explain why you chose what you did.

1. Had you been one of the Twelve, how would you have most likely dealt with this conflict?

   ☐ I would have told them to file a report.
   ☐ I would have ignored it and figured it would go away.
   ☐ I would have written them off as complainers and hoped they would leave the church.
   ☐ I would have tried to solve the problem directly myself.
   ☐ I would have delegated the problem to someone qualified, as the Twelve did.

2. Where do you see "cultural clashes" like this one in the church today? What needs to be done to get past cultural differences and encourage a fellowship that cares for one another?

3. Who is being neglected in your church today? What can you do to correct that situation?

life change lessons

How can you apply this session to your life?

1. Why is dropping out or leaving a church in conflict often an unhealthy option?

Write your answers here.

2. Why should you pray for those who have a different perspective than you?

Caring Time

15-20 minutes

Close by taking time to pray for one another and for your own special concerns. Begin by having each group member finish the sentence:

"The greatest challenge or conflict I see facing me in the weeks ahead will be ..."

Then pray for God's strength and direction in the midst of these challenges. Also, use the Prayer/Praise Report and pray for the requests and concerns listed.

Pray specifically for God to guide you to someone to invite for next week to fill the empty chair.

4

Reference Notes

Use these notes to gain further understanding of the text as you study on your own.

ACTS 6:1

Many elderly Jews who had lived most of their lives elsewhere in the empire came to live in Jerusalem for their final years. Those who were widowed, now far from home, were subject to poverty. It was these women who were being neglected.

Grecian Jews. These were Jews who came from outside Palestine and for whom Aramaic and Hebrew were relatively unknown languages. Their synagogue worship was also conducted in their native languages.

Hebraic Jews. These were native to the land who spoke Aramaic as their daily language. Since all the apostles were Hebraic Jews, it may be that they were naturally more sensitive and aware of the needs of those with whom they could easily communicate.

ACTS 6:2

wait on tables. Literally, "to serve tables." This does not refer to being a waiter. Since banking at the time was done by people sitting at a table, to "serve tables" was a figure of speech for handling financial transactions. While many groups use this passage as the basis for the office of deacon, there is no title given to these men. However, the Greek verb "to serve" is the root word from which the English word "deacon" comes.

The names of the men chosen strongly indicate that all seven were Greek-speaking Jews. They perhaps also served as a bridge between the apostles and the Greek-speaking Jews to help avoid further unintentional difficulties between the two groups.

Stephen. This man moves to center stage in chapter 7, where he becomes the first Christian martyr.

Philip. Like Stephen, Philip demonstrated gifts of evangelism not unlike those of the apostles (v. 8; 8:4-8; 21:8). Of the other men nothing more is known.

laid their hands on them. In the Old Testament the laying on of hands signified either a blessing (Gen. 48:14) or a commissioning (Num. 27:18,23).

priests. While the Sadducees controlled the priesthood, many of the priests, like Zechariah the father of John the Baptist (Luke 1:5-6), were sincerely devout men.

notes

notes

A Dramatic Conversion

Prepare for the Session

	READINGS	REFLECTIVE QUESTIONS
Monday	Acts 9:1–6	What answers are you seeking of Jesus today? What is He asking of you?
Tuesday	Acts 9:7–9	In what ways are you "blind" right now? To what is God seeking to open your eyes?
Wednesday	Acts 9:10–15	How are you letting fear come between you and others who are brothers and sisters in Christ?
Thursday	Acts 9:32–35	In what ways are you suffering from "paralysis"—not acting when you are needing to act? What needs to happen in order for you to be "healed"?
Friday	Acts 9:36–39	Were you to die, what would your family and friends remember most about you?
Saturday	Acts 9:40	What is dead inside of you that needs to be brought to life? How could faith help make you well?
Sunday	Acts 9:41	Whom do you need to "help to their feet" right now?

BIBLE STUDY
- to consider what happened when Jesus came and turned Saul's life around
- to get a better understanding of what happens in dramatic conversions like Saul's
- to take a look at the need for support from others after conversion

LIFE CHANGE
- to share our faith with at least one person we have previously seen as a "threat"
- to "adopt" a new Christian in our church (either as a class or as an individual)
- to encourage the starting of a Christian recovery group

Icebreaker

10-15 minutes

Forks in the Road. An oft-repeated Yogi Berra saying is, "When you come to a fork in the road—take it." Well, we all come to forks in the road of our life, and *probably* what Yogi Berra was trying to say is that when that happens we have to make a decision and go one way or the other. Use the following questions to share your reaction to forks in the road, both real and hypothetical. Go around the group on question 1 and let everyone share. Then go around again on question 2.

1. If you came to a fork in the road between the following options, which path would you take?

| being a famous entertainer | · | being a CEO of a big corporation |

| spending a summer in Europe | · | spending a summer landscaping my yard |

| traveling to Mars | · | retreating to a castle in Spain |

| spending a year exploring an archaeological site | · · · · · · · · · · · · · · · · · · | spending a year exploring America's great shopping malls |

2. Which of the following "forks in the road" did you have the hardest time "taking"?

the life of a   the life of a
"carefree" single · family person

small town life · big city life

following my dreams · · · · · · · · · · · · · · following a practical career

doing it "my way" · · · · · · · · · · · · · · · · · · doing it the Lord's way

Information to Remember: In the spaces provided, take note of information you will need as you participate in this group in the weeks to come.

PEOPLE:

1. A person in our group who has not been here in a while is:

2. Someone who has never come to this group, but who might enjoy it is:

EVENTS: An event that is coming up that I want to make sure I am part of is _____. It will be _____ (time) on _____ (date) at _____ (location).

And if I have time, I would also like to be part of _____. It will be _____ (time) on _____ (date) at _____ (location).

Bible Study

30-45 minutes

The Scripture for this week:

LEARNING FROM THE BIBLE

ACTS 9:1–19

¹Meanwhile, Saul was still breathing out murderous threats against the Lord's disciples. He went to the high priest ²and asked him for letters to the synagogues in Damascus, so that if he found any there who belonged to the Way, whether men or women, he might take them as prisoners to Jerusalem. ³As he neared Damascus on his journey, suddenly a light from heaven flashed around him. ⁴He fell to the ground and heard a voice say to him, "Saul, Saul, why do you persecute me?"

⁵"Who are you, Lord?" Saul asked.

"I am Jesus, whom you are persecuting," he replied. ⁶"Now get up and go into the city, and you will be told what you must do."

⁷"The men traveling with Saul stood there speechless; they heard the sound but did not see anyone. ⁸Saul got up from the ground, but when he opened his eyes he could see nothing. So they led him by the hand into Damascus. ⁹For three days he was blind, and did not eat or drink anything.

¹⁰In Damascus there was a disciple named Ananias. The Lord called to him in a vision, "Ananias!"

"Yes, Lord," he answered.

¹¹The Lord told him, "Go to the house of Judas on Straight Street and ask for a man from Tarsus named Saul, for he is praying. ¹²In a vision he has seen a man named Ananias come and place his hands on him to restore his sight."

¹³"Lord," Ananias answered, "I have heard many reports about this man and all the harm he has done to your saints in Jerusalem. ¹⁴And he has come here with authority from the chief priests to arrest all who call on your name."

¹⁵But the Lord said to Ananias, "Go! This man is my chosen instrument to carry my name before the Gentiles and their kings and before the people of Israel. ¹⁶I will show him how much he must suffer for my name."

¹⁷Then Ananias went to the house and entered it. Placing his hands on Saul, he said, "Brother Saul, the Lord—Jesus, who appeared to you on the road as you were coming here—has sent me so that you may see again and be filled with the Holy Spirit." ¹⁸Immediately, something like scales fell from Saul's eyes, and he could see again. He got up and was baptized, ¹⁹and after taking some food, he regained his strength.

...about today's session

A WORD
FROM THE
LEADER

Write your
answers
here.

1. What factors do some people say predetermine a person's life?

2. In what ways can Saul's conversion be important to us personally?

Identifying with the Story

◡ In
horseshoe
groups of 6–8,
explore
questions as
time allows.

1. Who were you most likely to "persecute" when you were in grade school or junior high?

   ☐ nerds   ☐ the opposite sex
   ☐ a younger brother or sister   ☐ kids of another culture
   ☐ an older brother or sister   ☐ my parents
   ☐ the fat kids   ☐ other:_____

2. If Christ were to meet you on the road and call you on the carpet for something you used to do in your younger years, what would it be?

3. In your own coming to Christ, who was the Ananias whom God used to help turn you around?

today's session

1. What effect should it have upon us that the Bible is so honest about its heroes?

5

45

2. What name was given to Christianity at this time?

3. What gave Saul the power to change?

4. What were some aspects of Saul's personality that may not have changed?

5. What evidence is there that Saul, later called Paul, may have had continuing vision problems?

6. In what way might Ananias have been an example to Paul in ministerial style?

Learning from the Story

♘ **In
horseshoe
groups of 6–8,
choose an
answer and
explain why
you chose
what you did.**

1. What do you believe motivated Saul in his zeal for persecuting Christians?

   ☐ a sincere desire to do what was right
   ☐ a desire to win political points with the high priest
   ☐ a need to quiet his own doubts by attacking divergent opinions
   ☐ a desire to win points with God
   ☐ other: _____

2. When Saul saw his vision on the road to Damascus, it was:

   ☐ an hallucination
   ☐ the result of a buildup of guilt
   ☐ an intervention of God
   ☐ a moment of intuitive insight

3. Had you been Ananias, and God called on you to go minister to Saul, how would you have responded?

- ☐ "Here am I, send ... him!"
- ☐ "I don't do charity cases."
- ☐ "Surely, Lord, you jest!"
- ☐ "And who will watch my back?"
- ☐ "If you say so, Lord."

life change lessons

How can you apply this session to your life?

1. What does a church that wants to model itself on the church of Acts need to believe?

Write your answers here.

2. Why is it important that we also believe in God's power to change us?

5

Caring Time
15-20 minutes

CARING TIME

☖ Remain in horseshoe groups of 6–8.

Remember that this time is to develop and express your care for each other by sharing personal prayer requests and praying for each other's needs. Begin by having each group member finish the sentence:

"Right now I need an Ananias to help me ..."

Then pray for God's strength to make these changes and to be an "Ananias" for each other. Also, use the Prayer/Praise Report and pray for the concerns listed.

Pray specifically for God to guide you to someone to bring next week to fill the empty chair.

Reference Notes

Use these notes to gain further understanding
of the text as you study on your own.

**ACTS
9:1**

breathing out murderous threats. This reflects the depth of Saul's obsessive hatred toward the Christians. After hearing Stephen's speech (7:1-53), he undoubtedly viewed the Christians as an antiestablishment, heretical sect determined to undermine the Law of God and the worship of the temple. His ability to carry out his threats of murder would certainly have been proscribed by Roman law, but apparently he and the Sanhedrin had some success in their program (26:10).

**ACTS
9:2**

letters. While the Sanhedrin had no formal authority outside of Judea, its prestige could influence elders in synagogues far from Jerusalem. In this case, the Sanhedrin asked the elders in Damascus to cooperate with Saul by allowing him to arrest as blasphemers those Christians who had fled from Jerusalem to Damascus and bring them for trial in Jerusalem. The Book of Maccabees speaks of the Sanhedrin requesting officials in Egypt to give them extradition rights over Palestinian law-breakers who had fled there.
Damascus. A city about 150 miles from Jerusalem. Luke has not told us how the church began among the sizable Jewish community in this important city, but Saul desired to expand his persecution there so that it might not spread any further. This incident reveals how central Saul was to the carrying out of this first wave of persecution: once he was converted, this persecution dissipated (9:31).
the Way. This phrase is unique to Acts as a name for Christianity (19:9,23; 22:4; 24:14,22). It may stem from Jesus' claim in John 14:6.

**ACTS
9:3**

a light from heaven flashed around him. The term is often used of lightning, indicating the brilliance of the light (Acts 26:13). Light (glory) is commonly connected with divine appearances (Luke 9:29; Rev. 1:14-16).

**ACTS
9:4**

why do you persecute me. The opposition Saul created for the church was really directed against its Head, Jesus, demonstrating the identity between Jesus and the church, His body (Luke 10:16). God is bringing Saul face-to-face with the fact that by his activities he is not honoring God, but resisting the One glorified by God.

**ACTS
9:9**

This profound experience shattered all of Saul's previous convictions. Humbled and blinded, he fasted as he awaited what Jesus would do next with him.

ACTS **9:10**	Apart from Paul's comment in Acts 22:12, nothing is known of Ananias.
ACTS **9:11–12**	The vision Ananias received was matched by one Saul had of his coming. This double-dream confirmation is also seen in the story of Peter and Cornelius (ch. 10). **Straight Street.** The street that is called Straight, where Saul's host lived, is still one of the main thoroughfares of Damascus. The house of Judas is traditionally located near its western end. Nothing is known of Judas.
ACTS **9:13–14**	**Lord.** This title for Jesus, highlighting His authority, is a common one in this account (vv. 5,11,13,15,17), and in Paul's writings. **saints.** Literally, "holy ones." This was a common term for Israel in the Old Testament. Ananias applies it to Christians, as does Paul in his letters. It means those people who are separated out for God. **all who call on your name.** This way of referring to Christians comes from Joel 2:32. In the Book of Joel it was God's name (Yahweh) that was to be called upon: the fact that the early Christians transferred this to Jesus is a clear indication of their belief in His divinity.
ACTS **9:15–16**	The Lord overruled Ananias with a final command to "Go!" and a description of what Saul's mission would be. **my chosen instrument.** Literally, "a choice vessel." Some images from the Old Testament form the context here. Israel was compared to a vessel in the hand of a potter, formed to perform the task for which the potter created it (Jer. 18:1-6). The Servant of Isaiah was God's chosen (Isa. 44:1): Saul (soon to be Paul) would carry on the mission of the Servant in terms of bringing the light to the Gentiles (Isa. 42:6; 49:6) and in sharing in his suffering.
ACTS **9:17–19**	**Brother Saul.** Without further question, Ananias affirms Saul as part of the family through the grace of Jesus. After laying hands on him, Saul's sight was restored; he was baptized (presumably by Ananias); and was filled with the Holy Spirit.

5

notes

Session

6

The Community Expands

Prepare for the Session

	READINGS	REFLECTIVE QUESTIONS
Monday	Acts 10:1-8	What might an angel of God say about your prayer life right now?
Tuesday	Acts 10:9-16	When has God showed you a new perspective on your beliefs? How did you respond?
Wednesday	Acts 10:17-23	How would your outreach to others be different if you truly believed that no person or group of persons was "unclean"?
Thursday	Acts 11:19-21	In what ways might God be calling you to go beyond your "comfort zone"?
Friday	Acts 11:22-24	Who has encouraged you lately? How can you encourage someone this week?
Saturday	Acts 11:25-26	Who has especially helped you in the work you do? How can you thank this person?
Sunday	Acts 11:27-30	In what area of your life are you experiencing a "famine"? How could your Christian brothers and sisters help you in the midst of this "famine"?

6

BIBLE STUDY

- to see how the Christian community of Acts expanded to include Gentiles
- to understand what it means for us today that we should not call anyone "impure or unclean"
- to acknowledge how the Christian community is strengthened by being multicultural

LIFE CHANGE

- to discover what cultural groups are present in the community, but are under-represented in the churches
- to invite someone from another culture into our homes
- to initiate a pulpit exchange, combined worship, or social function between our church and an ethnic church

Icebreaker

10-15 minutes

Uninvited. In the following questions, share the role "uninvited" persons have played in your life. Go around the group on question 1 and let everyone share. Then go around again on question 2.

1. What person or persons would you have seen as "uninvited" in your life when you were in high school?

   ☐ nerds
   ☐ Christian kids who kept trying to convert me
   ☐ the druggies
   ☐ a prodigal parent who didn't live with us
   ☐ kids of other racial groups
   ☐ adults in general
   ☐ other: _____

2. When has someone you considered to be "uninvited" broken through and become a significant part of your life?

Information to Remember: In the spaces provided, take note of information you will need as you participate in this group in the weeks to come.

PEOPLE:

1. A person in the group I would like to hear from more today is:

2. A person in the group whom God may be leading me to say something special to today is:

EVENTS: An event that is coming up that I want to make sure I am part of is _____. It will be _____ (time) on _____ (date) at _____ (location).

And if I have time, I would also like to be part of _____. It will be _____ (time) on _____ (date) at _____ (location).

Bible Study
30-45 minutes

The Scripture for this week:

LEARNING FROM THE BIBLE

ACTS 10:1–23

¹At Caesarea there was a man named Cornelius, a centurion in what was known as the Italian Regiment. ²He and all his family were devout and God-fearing; he gave generously to those in need and prayed to God regularly. ³One day at about three in the afternoon he had a vision. He distinctly saw an angel of God, who came to him and said, "Cornelius!"

⁴Cornelius stared at him in fear. "What is it, Lord?" he asked.

The angel answered, "Your prayers and gifts to the poor have come up as a memorial offering before God. ⁵Now send men to Joppa to bring back a man named Simon who is called Peter. ⁶He is staying with Simon the tanner, whose house is by the sea."

⁷When the angel who spoke to him had gone, Cornelius called two of his servants and a devout soldier who was one of his attendants. ⁸He told them everything that had happened and sent them to Joppa.

⁹About noon the following day as they were on their journey and approaching the city, Peter went up on the roof to pray. ¹⁰He became hungry and wanted something to eat, and while the meal was being prepared, he fell into a trance. ¹¹He saw heaven opened and something like a large sheet being let down to earth by its four corners. ¹²It contained all kinds of four-footed animals, as well as reptiles of the earth and birds of the air. ¹³Then a voice told him, "Get up, Peter. Kill and eat."

¹⁴"Surely not, Lord!" Peter replied. "I have never eaten anything impure or unclean."

¹⁵The voice spoke to him a second time, "Do not call anything impure that God has made clean."

¹⁶This happened three times, and immediately the sheet was taken back to heaven.

¹⁷While Peter was wondering about the meaning of the vision, the men sent by Cornelius found out where Simon's house was and stopped at the gate. ¹⁸They called out, asking if Simon who was known as Peter was staying there.

¹⁹While Peter was still thinking about the vision, the Spirit said to him, "Simon, three men are looking for you. ²⁰So get up and go downstairs. Do not hesitate to go with them, for I have sent them."

²¹Peter went down and said to the men, "I'm the one you're looking for. Why have you come?"

²²The men replied, "We have come from Cornelius the centurion. He is a righteous and God-fearing man, who is respected by all the Jewish people. A holy angel told him to have you come to his house so that he could hear what you have to say." ²³Then Peter invited the men into the house to be his guests.

...about today's session

A WORD FROM THE LEADER

1. What situations could one point to in support of the idea that we really can't "all get along"?

Write your answers here.

2. What is the key to turning former enemies into friends?

Identifying with the Story

In horseshoe groups of 6–8, explore questions as time allows.

1. If this were your vision, what kind of food would come down in the sheet?

   ☐ meat of any kind—I'm a vegetarian.
   ☐ raw oysters
   ☐ deer or game meat
   ☐ liver
   ☐ cow's tongue or brains
   ☐ meat of any kind—I'm a vegetarian.
   ☐ anything with artificial preservatives
   ☐ tofu or other "health food"
   ☐ the same things that were in Peter's sheet—I don't do reptiles!
   ☐ Nothing would be in it, because I'll eat anything!

2. When have you, like Peter, had a dream through which you suspected God might be trying to tell you something?

6

3. Which people or groups would God have to first open your heart to in a vision or dream before you would socialize with and witness to them?

   ☐ alcoholics or drug addicts   ☐ homeless people
   ☐ KKK or hate group members   ☐ homosexuals
   ☐ sexual offenders   ☐ prostitutes
   ☐ the wealthy country club set   ☐ ex-convicts
   ☐ people of another race or culture
   ☐ youth with spiked dog collars and tattoos
   ☐ other: _____

today's session

What is God teaching you from this story?

1. What was perhaps the biggest cultural division of biblical times?

2. Why did God originally want the people of Israel to separate themselves from the people around them?

3. Why would Cornelius have been especially hated?

4. Why does it seem a little strange that Cornelius was instructed to send for Peter? How did God use this situation to teach Peter?

5. At what times did devout Jews generally pray?

6. Why did Peter hesitate to follow the directions of the voice in his vision?

7. What is the central concept that Peter learned from this vision?

Learning from the Story

⊃ **In
horseshoe
groups of 6–8,
choose an
answer and
explain why
you chose
what you did.**

1. What impresses you most about Cornelius?

   ☐ Though raised in a polytheistic culture, he was committed to the one true God.

   ☐ Though a military man in an occupying force, he cared for the people.

   ☐ He was generous to the poor.

   ☐ He was obedient to the vision given to him.

2. Had you been Peter, what would have been going through your mind when you saw the vision of the animals in the sheet?

☐ "Is this some kind of trick of the Devil?"
☐ "Is God changing the rules in the middle of the game?"
☐ "I think I might not be so hungry after all!"
☐ "What is God trying to tell me?" _____

3. How would it change your behavior if you believed in your heart that all people were "clean"?

life change lessons

How can you apply this session to your life?

1. What does a church miss out on when its members only reach out to people of their own culture?

Write your answers here.

2. What is a good way to check out which cultural groups are present in your community?

6

Caring Time

15-20 minutes

CARING TIME

◊ Remain in horseshoe groups of 6–8.

Close by praying for one another. Begin this time by having each person answer the question,

"If you could receive an answer to just one question you are facing in your life, what would you want answered?"

Then pray for direction in regard to each other's questions. In addition, pray for the concerns on the Prayer/Praise Report.

Pray specifically for God to guide you to someone to bring next week to fill the empty chair.

Reference Notes

Use these notes to gain further understanding
of the text as you study on your own.

**ACTS
10:1**

Cornelius. The Romans typically used three names. Cornelius was a popular name taken on by the descendants of slaves who were released from slavery by the action of a P. Cornelius Sculla in 82 B.C. Cornelius would have been this soldier's middle name.

a centurion. Equivalent to the rank of an army captain in today's terms.
the Italian Regiment. An auxiliary force stationed in the area composed of men recruited from Italy.

**ACTS
10:2**

God-fearing. The distinction between Gentile God-fearers (who believed in the true God and obeyed His ethical commands) and proselytes (who fully converted to Judaism) lay in the hesitancy of the former to submit to the Jewish ceremonial laws, especially circumcision. Cornelius demonstrated his faith by practicing the Jewish disciplines of prayer and almsgiving.

**ACTS
10:3**

about three in the afternoon. This was the time for afternoon prayers at the temple in Jerusalem. Although Cornelius would never be able to participate fully in the temple services, he may have followed its pattern in terms of his own mode and time for prayer.

**ACTS
10:4**

Lord. Cornelius did not yet know of Jesus, so this is an expression of respect for what Cornelius recognized as a divine visitor.
as a memorial offering by God. Although Cornelius would not have been allowed to offer animal sacrifices in the temple, the angel lets him know that his heart-attitude of devotion to God is recognized as a real sacrifice that is acceptable to God.

**ACTS
10:5–8**

Told by the angel to send for Peter in Joppa, Cornelius sends three men to do so, at least one of whom shared his devotion to God.

**ACTS
10:9**

about noon. When apart from the temple, many devout Jews prayed at 9 a.m., noon, and 3 p.m. (Ps. 55:17).
up on the roof. Roofs were flat and often used as places for people to sit.

**ACTS
10:14**

Lord. Typically in Acts, this word is used as a title for Jesus. Peter may have recognized his dream as coming from the Lord, but he was not willing to simply follow the Lord's invitation to eat of the food.

**ACTS
10:15**

In Mark 7:19 Jesus laid the groundwork for the pronouncement that, despite the laws of Leviticus 11, food simply was not a spiritual issue. Such laws had their place earlier in Jewish history as a means of separating

ACTS 10:15 (cont'd) them from the pagans in neighboring areas, and as an object lesson about the meaning of holiness (that is, being separated out for God's use). (For an Old Testament story where eating became an issue for young Jewish men who sought to retain their cultural identity, read Daniel 1:3-17.) However, Jesus' point was to show that these object lessons were not to be mistaken as God's ultimate concern: his interest was in genuine, inward holiness that had nothing to do with external matters such as food, circumcision, etc. Demonstrating the reality of this was the burden of much of Paul's ministry (Rom. 2:25-29; 14:13-18; 1 Cor. 8:4-13; Gal. 4:8-11; 5:6; Phil. 3:2-9). Peter soon came to see that if God can pronounce that certain foods that were formerly unclean are now acceptable, he can do the same thing with people. If it is now acceptable for Jews to eat the food of Gentiles, then the Gentiles themselves must be considered as acceptable to God as well.

ACTS 10:18 *who was known as Peter.* Jesus had renamed Simon "Peter," meaning "rock," because Jesus had foreseen that he would be the rock upon which the church would be built (Matt. 16:17-19).

ACTS 10:19 *still thinking about the vision.* Peter was no doubt trying to determine what the vision meant in terms of actions he should or should not take. While he was seeking such direction, God sent him the answer in the form of the centurion's messengers.

6

ACTS 10:20 *I have sent them.* The deity of the Spirit is shown here in that He speaks for God in the first person.

ACTS 10:22 The men speak of Cornelius in a way to present him as favorably as possible to Peter. He is a God-fearer, respected by the Jews in his community. Since it would not be easy for a Roman to earn such Jewish respect, this was particularly impressive. What is more, an angel spoke to him about Peter, saying that he should listen to whatever Peter had to say to him. Thus prepared, Peter would have to be expectant that something especially important was about to occur.

ACTS 10:23 While Jews would offer Gentiles hospitality, they typically would refuse to accept it from Gentiles lest they violate dietary laws. Assuming the messengers arrived in early afternoon (v. 9), it would have been too late in the day to start the 30-mile journey back to Caesarea.

notes

A Praying Church

Prepare for the Session

	READINGS	REFLECTIVE QUESTIONS
Monday	Acts 12:1–4	In what ways are you like Herod, attempting to please the crowd?
Tuesday	Acts 12:5–11	From what has God rescued you? Whose prayers were part of helping this to happen?
Wednesday	Acts 12:12–17	In what frustrating areas of your life do you need to "keep on knocking"? How does God help you to persist in these circumstances?
Thursday	Acts 13:32–33	In what ways has God been faithful to His promises to you?
Friday	Acts 13:38–39	Meditate on how gracious God has been in forgiving you of your sins.
Saturday	Acts 13:49–52	In what ways do you need to "shake the dust" of a past failure from your feet and move on to what God is calling you to do next?
Sunday	Acts 14:1–3	How bold are you being in standing up for your Lord Jesus Christ?

BIBLE STUDY

- to better understand the role that prayer played in the early church
- to appreciate the power of prayer to change things in our world
- to consider what our expectations of prayer should be and how those expectations influence prayer's effect

LIFE CHANGE

- to ask two people outside of the group to share a time when God responded to their prayers in a seemingly miraculous way
- to pray each day this week about some seemingly "impossible" situation
- to submit a previous prayer disappointment to Christ's Lordship

Icebreaker

10-15 minutes

GATHERING THE PEOPLE ♘ Form horseshoe groups of 6–8.

An **Open Door.** Go around the group on question 1 and let everyone share. Then go around again on question 2.

1. When you were in high school, which of the following "open doors" were you likely to burst right through and which ones were you likely to miss entirely? Mark the ones you would have taken advantage of right away with a "+" and those you would have missed with a "–":

____ Someone gave me the perfect lead-in for a put-down joke.

____ An attractive person of the opposite sex hinted they were interested in me.

____ A teacher gave me a chance to improve my grade.

____ I was given special encouragement to try out for the school play.

____ A good summer job suddenly became available.

____ I was given a chance to become a foreign exchange student.

2. What door would you most like to see opened at this stage of your life?

☐ the door to a new career opportunity
☐ the door to a new friendship or love relationship
☐ the door to a promotion within my present career
☐ the door to an exciting travel opportunity
☐ the door to an exciting educational opportunity
☐ the door to a new understanding of myself
☐ other: _____

Information to Remember: Finish the following sentences as you look around at the people here today.

1. The person in the group who has the biggest smile today is:

2. The person in the group who looks like he or she could use a hug is:

Bible Study

30-45 minutes 7

The Scripture for this week:

LEARNING FROM THE BIBLE

ACTS 12:1–17

¹*It was about this time that King Herod arrested some who belonged to the church, intending to persecute them. ²He had James, the brother of John, put to death with the sword. ³When he saw that this pleased the Jews, he proceeded to seize Peter also. This happened during the Feast of Unleavened Bread. ⁴After arresting him, he put him in prison, handing him over to be guarded by four squads of four soldiers each. Herod intended to bring him out for public trial after the Passover.*

⁵*So Peter was kept in prison, but the church was earnestly praying to God for him.*

⁶*The night before Herod was to bring him to trial, Peter was sleeping between two soldiers, bound with two chains, and sentries stood guard at the entrance. ⁷Suddenly an angel of the Lord appeared and a light shone in the cell. He struck Peter on the side*

and woke him up. "Quick, get up!" he said, and the chains fell off Peter's wrists.

⁸Then the angel said to him, "Put on your clothes and sandals." And Peter did so. "Wrap your cloak around you and follow me." the angel told him. ⁹Peter followed him out of the prison, but he had no idea that what the angel was doing was really happening; he thought he was seeing a vision. ¹⁰They passed the first and second guards and came to the iron gate leading to the city. It opened for them by itself, and they went through it. When they had walked the length of one street, suddenly the angel left him.

¹¹Then Peter came to himself and said, "Now I know without a doubt that the Lord sent his angel and rescued me from Herod's clutches and from everything the Jewish people were anticipating."

¹²When this had dawned on him, he went to the house of Mary the mother of John, also called Mark, where many people had gathered and were praying. ¹³Peter knocked at the outer entrance, and a servant girl named Rhoda came to answer the door. ¹⁴When she recognized Peter's voice, she was so overjoyed she ran back without opening it and exclaimed, "Peter is at the door!"

¹⁵"You're out of your mind," they told her. When she kept insisting that it was so, they said, "It must be his angel."

¹⁶But Peter kept on knocking, and when they opened the door and saw him, they were astonished. ¹⁷Peter motioned with his hand for them to be quiet and described how the Lord had brought him out of prison. "Tell James and the brothers about this," he said, and then he left for another place.

...about today's session

A WORD
FROM THE
LEADER

Write your
answers
here.

1. What three different ways of looking at prayer are mentioned?

   a. _____

   b. _____

   c. _____

2. What example is given of a time in the Bible when God said "no" to an earnest prayer?

Identifying with the Story

⋃ In horseshoe groups of 6–8, explore questions as time allows.

1. When you were a child in grade school and you had a story to tell that was hard to believe, who would generally believe you when nobody else would?

☐ my mom   ☐ my dad
☐ a sibling   ☐ a grandparent
☐ a good friend   ☐ a special teacher

2. When has something happened to you that was so good you didn't know if it was real or if you were dreaming?

3. When has God surprised you with the way that He answered your prayers?

7

today's session

What is God teaching you from this story?

1. Why was this Herod persecuting the church?

2. Why was Herod waiting until after the Passover to deal with Peter?

3. Where did Peter go after he was released from prison?

4. What scriptural references are given to tell of the power of prayer?

5. What we need to do then, is to pray with the _____ that God can change things through our prayers, but also with the _____ of understanding that God knows what is best.

Learning from the Story

**✂ In
horseshoe
groups of 6–8,
choose an
answer and
explain why
you chose
what you did.**

1. Had you been Peter, which of the events of this story would you have found most surprising?

   ☐ That they had arrested you in the first place.
   ☐ That you were so miraculously freed from the prison.
   ☐ That Rhoda left you at the door instead of letting you in.
   ☐ other: _____

2. Why do you think God delivered Peter from prison, but not James (v. 2)?

   ☐ God had more need of Peter's leadership.
   ☐ The people prayed more for Peter.
   ☐ God just wanted to demonstrate His power and chose Peter to do it with.
   ☐ Peter had greater faith.
   ☐ other: _____

3. What do you think was the most important effect this event had on the life of the church in Jerusalem?

   ☐ They had a new belief in the power of prayer.
   ☐ They had a new confidence that the authorities couldn't defeat them.
   ☐ They were reassured that they were on "the right side."
   ☐ other: _____

life change lessons

How can you apply this session to your life?

Write your answers here.

1. What two extremes do we need to avoid regarding our attitude about prayer results?

2. During times when our prayers aren't answered in the way we want, what words from Eli, in the book of Samuel, are we called upon to repeat?

Caring Time

15-20 minutes

CARING TIME

◡ Remain in horseshoe groups of 6–8.

Take time now to care for one another through prayer. Begin by having each group member answer the following question:

"From what 'prison' do you need to be
released right now?"

Close by praying for one another. Also, use the Prayer/Praise Report and pray for the concerns and requests listed.

Pray specifically for God to guide you to someone to invite for next week to fill the empty chair.

Reference Notes

Use these notes to gain further understanding
of the text as you study on your own.

ACTS
12:1

King Herod. This is Herod Agrippa I, the grandson of Herod the Great, who ruled when Jesus was born, and the nephew of Herod Antipas who governed Galilee during Jesus' ministry. Herod Agrippa I was popular with the Jews; some even wondered if he might be the Messiah who would free them from Rome. To further cultivate this popularity, he resumed the persecution of the church, which had ceased upon Paul's conversion (9:31). Since Herod died in A.D. 44, this story precedes the visit of Paul and Barnabas to Jerusalem (11:27-30).

ACTS
12:7

a light shone. Similarities between this story and other escape stories circulating in the first century have led some commentators to assume that supernatural overtones were added to an account of how Peter was released with the help of a sympathetic insider. However, this fails to account for how the security measures used to imprison Peter could have been circumvented. Peter was constantly guarded by four soldiers on six-hour shifts (vv. 4,6). Two soldiers were in the cell with Peter chained to their wrists, while the other two stood guard at the door. Such intense security measures may have been implemented to prevent any such "unexplainable" release such as happened when the Sanhedrin had imprisoned him earlier (5:19-24). The description of the light, a common symbol of divine glory, underscores that this was a miraculous intervention of God.

ACTS
12:8–10

In a trance-like state, Peter was led past the prison's guard and through the main door of the prison.

ACTS
12:11

the Lord ... rescued me from Herod's clutches. In Acts, there is no predictable pattern of how God will work. While Peter was released from prison, James, for whom the church undoubtedly prayed just as earnestly, was killed. Dorcas, a kindly but relatively insignificant woman (9:36-41), is raised from the dead while a bold, courageous man like Stephen is not. Even in this account, Peter, although so miraculously protected by God, decides he should go into hiding lest Herod catch him again (v. 17). The answer to why these things should be so is not given. The mystery is only known in the secret counsel of God who works all things according to His will. The call to the church is to be faithful and take responsible action whether or not God chooses to act in a miraculous way.

ACTS 12:12

Mary the mother of John, also called Mark. This is the Mark who later wrote the Gospel bearing that name (12:25; 13:5).

ACTS 12:13–17

In a humorous way, Luke recounts how Peter was left standing at the gate of the courtyard while the disciples refused to believe that he could possibly be there!

ACTS 12:15

It must be his angel. It was believed that each person had a guardian angel who watched over that individual. Assuming that Peter was killed, the only solution the disciples could come up with was that Peter's angel had taken on Peter's form.

ACTS 12:17

James. This is the half-brother of Jesus (Mark 6:3). James did not believe in Jesus as the Messiah during Jesus' ministry (John 7:5), but after the resurrection Jesus appeared to him in a special way (1 Cor. 15:7), qualifying James to be an apostle. James became a leader in the Jerusalem church (15:13; 21:18; Gal. 2:9), and his piety and devotion to God gained the respect of the Jewish community in general. When executed by the Sadducean high priest in A.D. 61, his death was mourned by many Pharisaic Jews as well as Christians.

he left for another place. While Peter recognized his release as an act of God, he did not believe that made him invulnerable to Herod's plots. Thus, he left Jerusalem for some time. Although Peter was in Jerusalem at the time of the council in Acts 15, nothing more is told of his story in Acts. Church tradition associates him with travels to Alexandria, Asia Minor, and finally Rome where he was crucified upside down by the Emperor Nero.

7

notes

Treated as Gods

Prepare for the Session

	READINGS	REFLECTIVE QUESTIONS
Monday	Acts 14:8–10	Consider what "spiritual disabilities" you have at this point in your life. Do you have faith that God can heal you?
Tuesday	Acts 14:11–15	Have you made peace with the fact that you are only human?
Wednesday	Acts 14:16–18	How has God shown kindness to you? How have you thanked Him?
Thursday	Acts 14:19–20	When the world has seemingly turned against you, who has been there to help you pick up the pieces?
Friday	Acts 14:21–22	What hardships are you experiencing because you are seeking the kingdom of God? Who has encouraged you in the midst of those hardships?
Saturday	Acts 14:23–25	Is your trust truly in the Lord?
Sunday	Acts 14:26–28	For whom can you "open the door of faith"?

8

BIBLE STUDY

- to look at the human tendency to view certain charismatic leaders as "gods"
- to consider the humble way Paul and Barnabas dealt with the power given to them
- to understand how quickly people can change their minds about whom they idolize

LIFE CHANGE

- to review the stories of Jim Jones and David Koresh
- to make a list of positive and negative things you notice about Christian leaders in general
- to become part of or remain in a group where honesty and openness is encouraged

Icebreaker

10-15 minutes

**GATHERING
THE PEOPLE
◡ Form
horseshoe
groups of 6–8.**

This Week's Journey. Paul had many interesting experiences on his journeys. What about you? Imagine your journey this past week was a section of the trail that goes along a mountain range.

1. When did the "trail" seem so steep that you wished you could turn around and go back?

2. What beauty did you experience that made it, at least for the moment, seem all worthwhile?

3. Whom did you meet along the trail who made the hike the enjoyable?

4. What did you learn on this week's hike that will help you during the next few days of your trip?

Information to Remember: In the spaces provided, take note of information you will need as you participate in this group in the weeks to come. Finish the following sentences as you look around at the people here today.

PEOPLE:

1. A person in this group I might enjoy doing something with outside of class is:

2. A person who is not here who might enjoy a phone call is:

EVENTS: An event that is coming up that I want to make sure I am part of is _____. It will be _____ (time) on _____ (date) at _____ (location).

And if I have time, I would also like to be part of _____. It will be _____ (time) on _____ (date) at _____ (location).

Bible Study
30-45 minutes

The Scripture for this week:

LEARNING FROM THE BIBLE

ACTS 14:8-20

[8]*In Lystra there sat a man crippled in his feet, who was lame from birth and had never walked.* [9]*He listened to Paul as he was speaking. Paul looked directly at him, saw that he had faith to be healed* [10]*and called out, "Stand up on your feet!" At that, the man jumped up and began to walk.*

[11]*When the crowd saw what Paul had done, they shouted in the Lycaonian language, "The gods have come down to us in human form!"* [12]*Barnabas they called Zeus, and Paul they called Hermes because he was the chief speaker.* [13]*The priest of Zeus, whose temple was just outside the city, brought bulls and wreaths to the city gates because he and the crowd wanted to offer sacrifices to them.*

[14]*But when the apostles Barnabas and Paul heard of this, they tore their clothes and rushed out into the crowd, shouting:* [15]*"Men, why are you doing this? We too are only men, human like you. We are bringing you good news, telling you to turn from these worthless*

things to the living God, who made heaven and earth and sea and everything in them. [16]In the past, he let all nations go their own way. [17]Yet he has not left himself without testimony: He has shown kindness by giving you rain from heaven and crops in their seasons; he provides you with plenty of food and fills your hearts with joy." [18]Even with these words, they had difficulty keeping the crowd from sacrificing to them.

[19]Then some Jews came from Antioch and Iconium and won the crowd over. They stoned Paul and dragged him outside the city, thinking he was dead. [20]But after the disciples had gathered around him, he got up and went back into the city. The next day he and Barnabas left for Derbe.

...about today's session

1. What ancient peoples deified their leaders?

2. What leader in recent times did people treat like a "god?"

Identifying with the Story

1. When you were in school, who were you most likely to think of as "gods"?

   ☐ baseball players like Mickey Mantle, Willie Mays, George Brett, or Pete Rose

   ☐ basketball players like Wilt Chamberlain, Larry Bird, or Michael Jordan

   ☐ football players like Gayle Sayers, Joe Montana, John Elway, or Emmitt Smith

   ☐ singers like Elvis Presley, Aretha Franklin, Prince, or Madonna

   ☐ actors like Gregory Peck, John Wayne, Jane Fonda, Harrison Ford, or Julia Roberts

   ☐ political leaders like Bobby Kennedy, Ronald Reagan, Geraldine Ferraro, or Diane Feinstein

   ☐ religious leaders like Billy Graham, Rick Warren, Mother Teresa, or the Pope

2. Finish this sentence: "The last time I felt I was really treated 'like a god' was when ..."

3. In general, do you feel people treat you better than you deserve, as the Lycaonians did with Paul and Barnabas at first; or worse than you deserve, as they treated Paul and Barnabas after the Jewish instigators came along?

∞∞∞ today's session

What is God teaching you from this story?

1. According to local legend, what two Greek gods had already come down to earth in this region in human form?

2. Why didn't Paul and Barnabas understand at first that they were being thought of as gods come to earth in human form?

3. Why did Paul and Barnabas tear their clothes?

4. After they realize that they are being thought of as gods, what three points do Paul and Barnabas make to the crowd?

   a. _____

   b. _____

   c. _____

5. To what does Paul Tournier liken those who try to function without the direction of their Creator?

6. What are we encouraged to do instead of relying on one "god-like" charismatic leader?

75

Learning from the Story

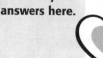 In horseshoe groups of 6–8, choose an answer and explain why you chose what you did.

1. Why was the crowd that had previously proclaimed Paul and Barnabas as gods so quickly persuaded to stone them?

2. Why were Paul and Barnabas so upset when they realized the crowd was getting ready to offer sacrifices to them?

   ☐ They thought God might punish them.
   ☐ They knew God alone was worthy of such behavior.
   ☐ People weren't listening to their message about Jesus.
   ☐ They didn't want people expecting too much of them.
   ☐ other:_____

3. What do you see as the most significant message Barnabas and Saul sought to deliver to the crowd?

   ☐ There is one living God for all people (v. 15).
   ☐ God is the Creator of everything (v. 15).
   ☐ God had always reached out to them (v. 17).
   ☐ God provided for them materially (v. 17).
   ☐ God provided for them spiritually and emotionally (v. 17).

life change lessons

How can you apply this session to your life?

Write your answers here.

1. "We need to let people be _____."

2. What might be one possible reason that some people see only the negative in others?

Caring Time
15-20 minutes

CARING TIME

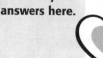 Remain in horseshoe groups of 6–8.

Take this time to encourage one another in prayer. Begin by having each group member answer the question:

"What has God done recently that has 'filled your heart with joy' (v. 17)?"

Thank God for these things in prayer. In addition, pray for the concerns on the Prayer/Praise Report.

Pray specifically for God to guide you to someone to invite for next week to fill the empty chair.

Reference Notes

Use these notes to gain further understanding
of the text as you study on your own.

BIBLE
STUDY
NOTES

**ACTS
14:8**

The small Jewish community in Lystra (16:1-3) apparently did not have a synagogue. Adopting a new strategy that brought the gospel directly to the Gentiles, Paul probably preached in the Greek forum, the site of the local marketplace and gathering place for public discussion.

**ACTS
14:11**

An ancient legend said that Jupiter and Mercury (the Latin counterparts to Zeus and Hermes) appeared to a couple in a nearby area. As a result, the local people made pilgrimages to this site and the worship of these gods flourished in the region through the third century A.D.

**ACTS
14:12**

Hermes ... the chief speaker. Zeus was the chief god among the Greek deities, while Hermes was the herald of the gods. The fact that Paul was identified with Hermes shows that he was the leading speaker in this missionary enterprise.

**ACTS
14:14**

they tore their clothes. In the ancient world, this was a universally recognized sign of horror and grief. By so doing, the missionaries demonstrate the intensity of their opposition to what the people were supposedly doing in their honor.

**ACTS
14:15–17**

Paul declares that he and Barnabas are in no way divine, but only human messengers bringing a message from the one true, living God.

**ACTS
14:19–20**

Although there was not a sufficient Jewish community in Lystra to cause any opposition, some traditional Jewish zealots who had traveled from Antioch (over 150 miles away) and Iconium reflected Paul's former zeal in opposing the gospel by traveling to Lystra to stir up the people against him.

**ACTS
14:20**

he got up. While some consider this a miracle or resurrection, Luke gives no indication that this was so. Paul was badly beaten and bruised, but able to travel on to Derbe. Paul refers to this incident in 2 Corinthians 11:25 with no mention of any miraculous resurrection or recovery.

8

notes

9

Dealing with the Old Laws

Prepare for the Session

	READINGS	REFLECTIVE QUESTIONS
Monday	Acts 15:1–5	What "law" do you still feel you need to fulfill to "measure up"? How completely has God's grace struck home to you?
Tuesday	Acts 15:6–11	When was the last time you told someone what God has done for you and through you? Who could you tell today?
Wednesday	Acts 15:12–21	In what way is your lifestyle making it easier, or more difficult, for others to believe?
Thursday	Acts 15:24–29	What have you risked for Jesus Christ?
Friday	Acts 15:30–35	To whom have you given an encouraging message recently? To whom do you need to give an encouraging message?
Saturday	Acts 15:36	What Christian brother or sister do you need to contact and "see how they are doing"? Should you call, send a letter, or e-mail?
Sunday	Acts 15:37–41	How are you doing at giving others a second chance?

9

BIBLE STUDY

- to consider the importance of the controversy over circumcision in the early church
- to gain a better understanding of the place of Old Testament laws and traditions
- to appreciate how the controversy over circumcision was dealt with, and its implications for handling church conflict

LIFE CHANGE

- to interview our pastor or other influential church teacher on the role of Old Testament law and tradition in the life of the Christian
- to talk with a friend and discover his understanding of Old Testament law
- to write out a statement of our own view on the applicability of Old Testament law for the Christian

Icebreaker

10-15 minutes

GATHERING THE PEOPLE
♆ **Form horseshoe groups of 6–8.**

House Rules. Go around the group on question 1 and let everyone share. Then go around again on question 2.

1. What were some of the "house rules," written and unwritten, in the home where you were raised?

- ☐ "Don't rock the boat."
- ☐ "Father knows best!"
- ☐ "If Mom ain't happy; ain't nobody happy!"
- ☐ "Don't talk to others about family business."
- ☐ "Don't talk back."
- ☐ "Don't run in the house."
- ☐ "Children should be seen and not heard."
- ☐ "Clean up after yourself."
- ☐ "You use it; you put it away."
- ☐ "Don't say, 'Shut up!' "
- ☐ "Do what you want, but stay out of my way."
- ☐ "Walk softly when Dad's home."

2. What was your attitude toward "house rules" when you were an adolescent? Rate yourself on the following scale:

1 · · · · · · · · · 2 · · · · · · · · · 3 · · · · · · · · · 4 · · · · · · · · · 5

My parents said
"jump," and I
said, "How high?"

Whatever my
parents said,
I did the opposite.

Information to Remember: In the spaces provided, take note of information you will need as you participate in this group in the weeks to come.

PEOPLE:

1. A person here I would like to hear from more today is:

2. A person here whom God may be leading me to say something special to today is:

EVENTS: An event that is coming up that I want to make sure I am part of is _____. It will be _____ (time) on _____ (date) at _____ (location).

And if I have time, I would also like to be part of _____. It will be _____ (time) on _____ (date) at _____ (location).

Bible Study
30-45 minutes

9

The Scripture for this week:

LEARNING FROM THE BIBLE

ACTS 15:1–21

¹*Some men came down from Judea to Antioch and were teaching the brothers: "Unless you are circumcised, according to the custom taught by Moses, you cannot be saved."* ²*This brought Paul and Barnabas into sharp dispute and debate with them. So Paul and Barnabas were appointed, along with some other believers, to go up to Jerusalem to see the apostles and elders about this question.* ³*The church sent them on their way, and as they traveled through Phoenicia and Samaria they told how the Gentiles had been converted.*

This news made all the brothers very glad. ⁴When they came to Jerusalem, they were welcomed by the church and the apostles and elders, to whom they reported everything God had done through him.

⁵Then some of the believers who belonged to the party of the Pharisees stood up and said, "The Gentiles must be circumcised and required to obey the law of Moses."

⁶The apostles and elders met to consider this question. ⁷After much discussion, Peter got up and addressed them: "Brothers, you know that some time ago God made a choice among you that the Gentiles might hear from my lips the message of the gospel and believe. ⁸God, who knows the heart, showed that he accepted them by giving the Holy Spirit to them, just as he did to us. ⁹He made no distinction between us and them, for he purified their hearts by faith. ¹⁰Now then, why do you try to test God by putting on the necks of the disciples a yoke that neither we nor our fathers have been able to bear? ¹¹No! We believe it is through the grace of our Lord Jesus that we are saved, just as they are."

¹²The whole assembly became silent as they listened to Barnabas and Paul telling about the miraculous signs and wonders God had done among the Gentiles through them. ¹³When they finished, James spoke up: "Brothers, listen to me. ¹⁴Simon has described to us how God at first showed his concern by taking from the Gentiles a people for himself. ¹⁵The words of the prophets are in agreement with this, as it is written:

> ¹⁶" 'After this I will return
> and rebuild David's fallen tent.
> Its ruins I will rebuild,
> and I will restore it,
> ¹⁷that the remnant of men may seek the Lord,
> and all the Gentiles who bear my name,
> says the Lord, who does these things'
> ¹⁸that have been known for ages.

¹⁹"It is my judgment, therefore, that we should not make it difficult for the Gentiles who are turning to God. ²⁰Instead we should write to them, telling them to abstain from food polluted by idols, from sexual immorality, from the meat of strangled animals and from blood. ²¹For Moses has been preached in every city from the earliest times and is read in the synagogues on every Sabbath."

...about today's session

A WORD FROM THE LEADER

Write your answers here.

1. What example is given of a law that now seems trivial because it no longer serves its original function?

2. Why was it important in Old Testament times for Jewish men to have a sign that they were different from men of other cultures?

Identifying with the Story

◡ **In horseshoe groups of 6–8, explore questions as time allows.**

1. What is most likely to cause "sharp disputes" in your church?
   - ☐ theological issues—like how to apply Scripture
   - ☐ worship music disputes—guitars vs. organ
   - ☐ personality issues—pro-pastor vs. anti-pastor
   - ☐ matters of church decor—like the color of the carpet
   - ☐ power struggles—"us" vs. "them"

2. In matters of church dispute, what is your most frequent approach?
   - ☐ "Let's not talk about anything that will make people mad."
   - ☐ "If they don't straighten up, I'll leave!"
   - ☐ "You have a right to your opinion—even if it is wrong!"
   - ☐ "Let's agree to disagree."
   - ☐ "As long as we keep talking and listening, we'll figure it out."
   - ☐ other: _____

3. What church dispute has disturbed you the most?

9

What is God teaching you from this story?

1. What did the meeting at Jerusalem later become known as?

2. What creeds came out of later church councils?

3. How was it possible that people who believed in Jesus Christ could still consider themselves to be Pharisees?

4. Who is it that seems to make the decision to not force circumcision?

5. What four things does this Council ask Gentile converts not to do?

    a. _____

    b. _____

    c. _____

    d. _____

6. Did the decision of this First Church Council completely solve the conflict over circumcision? Support your answer.

Learning from the Story

In horseshoe groups of 6–8, choose an answer and explain why you chose what you did.

1. What were the most important factors in solving this conflict? Rate each of the following factors from 1 (unimportant) to 5 (vital):

    ____ They openly expressed their opinions (vv. 1-2).
    ____ They appealed to respected authorities (v. 2).
    ____ They allowed much discussion rather than having one or two persons make a quick decision (v. 7).
    ____ They were sensitive to the Holy Spirit (vv. 8,12).

2. To what degree do you see what happened as a result of democratic deliberation; and to what degree do you see it as imposed by authorities? Mark the scale below:

1 · · · · · · · · · 2 · · · · · · · · · 3 · · · · · · · · · 4 · · · · · · · · · 5
Democratic   Authoritarian

3. What implication does this incident have for the role of Old Testament law in the life of a Christian?

☐ It's all obsolete.
☐ Laws were kept or discarded by political compromise.
☐ The essential thing is faith in Christ—laws are secondary to that.
☐ God changed some laws that were unique to the Jews—all others remain.
☐ other: _____

life change lessons

How can you apply this session to your life?

1. What are some Old Testament laws and traditions that still cause debate among Christians today?

Write your answers here.

2. What are some specific issues we should discuss with our pastor?

Caring Time
15-20 minutes

9

CARING TIME

Use this time to pray for one another. Begin by having each group member answer the following question:

"With what conflict (internal or interpersonal) could you use prayer support right now?"

🐴 Remain in horseshoe groups of 6–8.

Then pray for these conflicts. Remember to use the Prayer/Praise Report and pray for the requests and concerns listed.

Pray specifically for God to guide you to someone to invite for next week to fill the empty chair.

Reference Notes

Use these notes to gain further understanding
of the text as you study on your own.

**ACTS
15:1-35**

Right in the middle of Luke's account is this record of the council in Jerusalem that met to discuss the status of Gentiles in the church. This critical meeting of the church marked its first self-conscious departure from orthodox Judaism. Had the council decided to support the claims of the Jewish believers, Christianity would have remained only another sect within Judaism.

**ACTS
15:1-4**

The controversy surrounding circumcision stirred up such a debate that the church felt it necessary to call together the recognized leaders from Jerusalem and Antioch to settle the issue. This is considered to be the First Church Council.

**ACTS
15:5**

the believers who belonged to the party of the Pharisees. The resistance to allowing Gentiles into the church originated with Jewish Christians who had formerly been Pharisees. This small but influential sect was widely respected for its adherence to the Law and traditions. Their concern arose from a genuine desire to insure that God's honor was not violated through disregard of His Law. To them, the offer of the gospel apart from the Law was inconceivable since for centuries their people had been taught to look to the Law to discern God's will. Paul's ministry seemed like a slap in Israel's face—an unthinkable rejection of all the covenant responsibilities of God's chosen people.

**ACTS
15:7-8**

As part of the discussion, Peter recounts his experience with Cornelius, which may have occurred ten or more years earlier (Acts 10:1–11:18). The fact that Cornelius experienced the presence of the Spirit in the same way the disciples did was proof to him that God accepted the Gentiles quite apart from the practice of Jewish law.

**ACTS
15:9-11**

It is by faith in Jesus that one is made pure by God. The fact that it has to be that way is made plain by the fact that neither Israel as a nation nor any Jew as an individual ever managed to live up to all the demands of the Law. This affirmation of God's intent to save Gentiles through faith in Jesus is Peter's last statement in Acts.

**ACTS
15:13-21**

James was the leader of the Jerusalem church, and the ultimate decision as to the position of the Jerusalem church was his to make. Since in Galatians 2:11–13 James appears to have represented those who believed that Gentiles could not be considered equal members of the church with

Jews, it may be that this council was the turning point when he realized the scope of Jesus' mission. James' affirmation of God's plan to save all types of people through faith in Jesus is his last statement in Acts as well.

ACTS
15:15

the words of the prophets. James' quote is primarily rooted in the Septuagint version of Amos 9:11–12. The Old Testament books of Hosea through Malachi were contained on a single scroll. To quote one was to assume the support of the others.

ACTS
15:16-18

The original context of the prophecy was the anticipation of the destruction of Israel (722 B.C.) after which God would one day return the nation to its former glory as in David's day. James sees that the way God is rebuilding "David's ... tent" (a symbol of God's presence with Israel) is by establishing His church, made up of all types of people who seek God. The differences between the Septuagint version quoted here and what is found in our Old Testament are a result of adding a *d* to the Hebrew word *yiresu* (possessing) to obtain *yirdresu* (seeking), and a dispute about whether the Hebrew word *dm* should be vocalized as *Edom* (the name of a country south of Israel) or as *adam* (the Hebrew word for humanity). In either case, the point is that God's new people will include Gentiles as well as Jews.

ACTS
15:20

telling them to abstain. These considerations sum up the Law in Leviticus 17–27 that applied to Israel and all foreigners who lived within her borders. *food polluted by idols.* In Gentile areas meat was sold only after the animal had been sacrificed as part of a worship service to an idol. The eating of such food was later to be a source of controversy between Jewish and Gentile believers in Rome (Rom. 14:1-8) and Corinth (1 Cor. 8). *sexual immorality.* This may be related to "the pollution of idols" since idolatry sometimes involved ritual prostitution (1 Cor. 6:12-20). *meat of strangled animals and from blood.* Jews were forbidden to eat meat that had any blood in it (Lev. 17:10-14). Gentiles would make the sharing of meals with Jewish believers easier if they would respect this tradition.

9

notes

10

A Spirit-Led Journey

Prepare for the Session

	READINGS	REFLECTIVE QUESTIONS
Monday	Acts 16:6–10	Who is God calling you to help right now? In what ways can you be of help to this person?
Tuesday	Acts 16:11–15	Do you have the gift of hospitality? If so, in what ways can you use it more to the glory of God?
Wednesday	Acts 16:25–31	What brought you to a realization that you needed to be saved? Take time to praise God for His grace.
Thursday	Acts 16:32–34	Do you still have the joy you first felt when you came to Christ? If so, how are you expressing that joy? If not, how can joy be restored to your life?
Friday	Acts 17:1–4	Are you maintaining a habit of regular worship? Are you an active part of what happens, or are you just an observer?
Saturday	Acts 17:5–9	Do you try to "not make waves," or are you willing to "rock the boat" when it is necessary?
Sunday	Acts 17:10–12	Are you examining the Scriptures regularly? If so, how is that discipline changing you?

10

BIBLE STUDY   • to appreciate the role of the Holy Spirit in
               directing Paul's path in his mission work
             • to see how Christian faith first came to
               Europe
             • to consider how the Holy Spirit's guidance
               can be discerned

LIFE CHANGE   • to provide for a "life direction evaluation
               period" during the coming week
             • to begin each day with prayer
             • to not overload our agenda

Icebreaker

10-15 minutes

Travel Plans. Go around the group on question 1, letting everyone
share. Then do the same with questions 2 and 3.

1. If you could travel to any country in the world for a visit, where
   would you want to go?

2. Who, besides immediate family, would you choose as traveling
   companions?

3. If money were no object, which of the following would be your
   preferred mode of travel?

   ☐ private jet   ☐ a private yacht
   ☐ a chauffeur-driven limo ☐ a luxury cruise liner
   ☐ a train with a private berth
   ☐ a luxury RV, with all the conveniences of home

Information to Remember: Finish the following sentences as you
look around at the people here today.

1. The person in the group today whom I know the least is:

2. Something I could do to get to know this person better is:

Bible Study

30-45 minutes

The Scripture for this week:

⁶*Paul and his companions traveled throughout the region of Phrygia and Galatia, having been kept by the Holy Spirit from preaching the word in the province of Asia.* ⁷*When they came to the border of Mysia, they tried to enter Bithynia, but the Spirit of Jesus would not allow them to.* ⁸*So they passed by Mysia and went down to Troas.* ⁹*During the night Paul had a vision of a man of Macedonia standing and begging him, "Come over to Macedonia and help us."* ¹⁰*After Paul had seen the vision, we got ready at once to leave for Macedonia, concluding that God had called us to preach the gospel to them.*

¹¹*From Troas we put out to sea and sailed straight for Samothrace, and the next day on the Neapolis.* ¹²*From there we traveled to Philippi, a Roman colony and the leading city of that district of Macedonia. And we stayed there several days.*

¹³*On the Sabbath we went outside the city gate to the river, where we expected to find a place of prayer. We sat down and began to speak to the women who had gathered there.* ¹⁴*One of those listening was a woman named Lydia, a dealer in purple cloth from the city of Thyatira, who was a worshiper of God. The Lord opened her heart to respond to Paul's message.* ¹⁵*When she and the members of her household were baptized, she invited us to her home. "If you consider me a believer in the Lord," she said, "come and stay at my house." And she persuaded us.*

10

...about today's session

**A WORD
FROM THE
LEADER**

**Write your
answers
here.**

1. What poet is mentioned as one who chose between two diverging paths? What basis did this person use for making his choice of path?

2. How did Paul's method of choosing which path to take differ from the poet's?

Identifying with the Story

1. When have unforeseen obstacles necessitated a change in plans for you?

2. How do you generally react when you have to make a change in plans (a long-planned vacation is delayed, rain cancels the picnic, etc.)?

☐ "Que sera, sera!"   ☐ A little irritated, but able to adapt.
☐ A total "basket-case"!   ☐ Really upset for a while.

3. When has a change in plans brought an unexpected "serendipity" into your life?

today's session

1. Name at least three important actions of the Holy Spirit in Acts:

   a. _____

   b. _____

   c. _____

2. In what town in the province of Asia did Paul later have a very successful mission?

3. What events may Paul have interpreted as meaning that the Holy Spirit or Spirit of Christ did not want him going into Asia or Bithynia? What vision redirected his path?

4. What do scholars believe is the significance of the change from "they" to "we" in the narrative of Acts?

5. Who seems to have been the first convert in Europe?

6. What business did this convert have, and why was it particularly lucrative?

Learning from the Story

In horseshoe groups of 6–8, choose an answer and explain why you chose what you did.

1. Why did Paul have such a strong sense of the Holy Spirit's guidance?

☐ He was Paul, a saint—God spoke more directly to him.
☐ It was one of his gifts—like being a psychic.
☐ He prayed for the Spirit's guidance, and kept open to that guidance.
☐ He didn't—it was just his way of interpreting coincidences.
☐ other: _____

2. Had Paul *not* been sensitive to the Spirit's guidance, how would it have affected the conversion of Lydia in particular and Europe in general? Would God have just found another way?

3. What obstacles do you see ahead of you in your present life path? Are these obstacles just normal obstacles that come to life, or are these obstacles God's way of telling you to take another direction? How can you tell?

life change lessons

**How can you
apply this
session to
your life?**

1. How does rushing around make it difficult for you to be in touch with the Holy Spirit?

**Write your
answers
here.**

2. Why is it sometimes difficult to evaluate what it means when you encounter obstacles in the way of your goals?

Caring Time

15–20 minutes

**CARING
TIME**

**🧲 Remain
in horseshoe
groups of 6–8.**

Close by sharing prayer requests and praying for one another. Begin by having each member of the group finish the sentence:

> *"Right now I am seeking the guidance
> of the Holy Spirit to ..."*

Then pray for these needs for guidance. In addition, pray for the concerns on the Prayer/Praise Report.

Pray specifically for God to guide you to someone to invite for next week to fill the empty chair.

Reference Notes

Use these notes to gain further understanding
of the text as you study on your own.

**ACTS
16:6–7**

the Holy Spirit ... the Spirit of Jesus. Luke clearly identifies the ongoing work of Jesus with the agency of the Holy Spirit in the lives of the apostles.

**ACTS
16:7**

would not allow them to. Why Jesus would not allow Paul and Silas to preach in Asia and Bithyna is not given. Later on, the Apostle Peter was in contact with churches in that area so they were not left bereft of the gospel (1 Peter 1:1).

**ACTS
16:8**

Troas. An important seaport on the Aegean Sea. While it appears Paul did not do any evangelistic work here at this time, he did do so later on (2 Cor. 2:12).

**ACTS
16:9**

Macedonia. This area of northern Greece had been the dominant power under Alexander the Great in the fourth century B.C.

**ACTS
16:10**

we. Verses 10–17 is the first of the passages written in the first person (20:5–21:18; 27:1–28:16), indicating that Luke himself was accompanying Paul at these points.

**ACTS
16:11–12**

In two days they arrived at Macedonia, landing at Neapolis. Philippi was a short distance to the west.

**ACTS
16:12**

the leading city of that district. The Greek here is uncertain. Since Philippi was neither the largest city nor the capital of the province, it probably should read simply, "a city of the first district of Macedonia." Macedonia was a Roman province divided into four districts.

**ACTS
16:13**

Ten men were required in order to form a synagogue. The fact that there was no synagogue in Philippi indicates how small the Jewish population was. *outside the city gate to the river.* The Jews may have been forbidden to meet inside the city limits, or they may have wanted to be near a river to perform their ceremonial washings.

**ACTS
16:14**

Lydia. Macedonian women enjoyed far more freedom and opportunities than many of their counterparts elsewhere. Lydia was a businesswoman involved in selling purple cloth, a luxury item indicating that she was a woman of wealth.
Thyatira. A city in the province of Asia noted for its dyeing industry. Evidence indicates that there was a Jewish community in Thyatira, which probably influenced Lydia toward faith in the God of the Jews. Lydia demonstrated her faith in Jesus as the Messiah by baptism and by offering hospitality to the missionaries.

10

**ACTS
16:15**

the members of her household. It was customary for children and servants to embrace the faith of their master or mistress (Acts 11:14).

notes

Speaking the
Language of the Culture

Prepare for the Session

	READINGS	REFLECTIVE QUESTIONS
Monday	Acts 17:16–21	What is distressing you the most about the society in which you are living? How well are you dealing with that stress?
Tuesday	Acts 17:22–28	In what ways might you be subjecting God to human limitations? What would it mean for you to expand your vision of Him?
Wednesday	Acts 17:29–34	How well do you handle the cynicism of others concerning the beliefs you hold dear?
Thursday	Acts 18:9–11	To what degree are you allowing fear to keep you from speaking up for your faith?
Friday	Acts 18:18–22	How much do you let God help you plan your itinerary as you go from place to place in your life?
Saturday	Acts 18:23–26	How receptive to correction are you? If God wanted to speak through some one else to change a misconception you have, would you be willing to listen?
Sunday	Acts 18:27–28	How is God using you right now to help other believers?

11

BIBLE STUDY
- to evaluate Paul's message and evangelistic method in Athens
- to consider how to keep gospel truth, while adapting methods to speak to different cultures
- to learn how to challenge the "gods" of a culture

LIFE CHANGE
- to discover one song of youth culture that proclaims a positive value
- to find a distinctive subculture in our town and learn what this subculture values
- to discover how our worship services can speak to the youth culture

Icebreaker

10-15 minutes

GATHERING THE PEOPLE ♘ **Form horseshoe groups of 6–8.**

My Sanity Defense. Go around the group on question 1 and have everyone answer. Then go around again on question 2.

1. If someone were to put you on trial to accuse you of not being sane, to what evidence would they likely point?

   ☐ I have volunteered to chaperone teenagers.
   ☐ I volunteered to teach my teenager how to drive.
   ☐ I once walked between a group of men and a TV when they were watching the Super Bowl.
   ☐ I have driven a car in Europe.
   ☐ I once invited my in-laws to live with us for a while.
   ☐ other: _____

2. Which of the following songs best describe what you would anticipate the outcome of the trial to be? (Put an "X" on the continuum to show which you would be closest to.)

"You may be right;
I may be crazy?"
(Billy Joel) ·
"I'm All Right"
(Kenny Loggins)

Information to Remember: In the spaces provided, take note of information you will need as you participate in this group in the weeks to come.

PEOPLE:

1. The person in our group who has not been here in a while is:

2. Someone who has never come to this group, but who might enjoy it is:

EVENTS: An event that is coming up that I want to make sure I am part of is _____. It will be _____ (time) on _____ (date) at _____ (location).

And if I have time, I would also like to be part of _____. It will be _____ (time) on _____ (date) at _____ (location).

Bible Study
30-45 minutes

The Scripture for this week:

LEARNING FROM THE BIBLE

ACTS 17:16–34

[16]While Paul was waiting for them in Athens, he was greatly distressed to see that the city was full of idols. [17]So he reasoned in the synagogue with the Jews and the God-fearing Greeks, as well as in the marketplace day by day with those who happened to be there. [18]A group of Epicurean and Stoic philosophers began to dispute with him. Some of them asked, "What is this babbler trying to say?" Others remarked, "He seems to be advocating foreign gods." They said this because Paul was preaching the good news about Jesus and the resurrection. [19]Then they took him and brought him to a meeting of the Areopagus, where they said to him, "May we know what this new teaching is that you are presenting? [20]You are bringing some strange ideas to our ears, and we want to know what they mean." [21](All the Athenians and the foreigners who lived there spent their time doing nothing but talking about and listening to the latest ideas.)

11

²²Paul then stood up in the meeting of the Areopogus and said: "Men of Athens! I see that in every way you are very religious. ²³For as I walked around and looked carefully at your objects of worship, I even found an altar with this inscription: TO AN UNKNOWN GOD. Now what you worship as something unknown I am going to proclaim to you.

²⁴"The God who made the world and everything in it is the Lord of heaven and earth and does not live in temples built by hands. ²⁵And he is not served by human hands, as if he needed anything, because he himself gives all men life and breath and everything else. ²⁶From one man he made every nation of men, that they should inhabit the whole earth; and he determined the times set for them and the exact places where they should live. ²⁷God did this so that men would seek him and perhaps reach out for him and find him, though he is not far from each one of us. ²⁸'For in him we live and move and have our being.' As some of your own poets have said, 'We are his offspring.'

²⁹"Therefore since we are God's offspring, we should not think that the divine being is like gold or silver or stone—an image made by man's design and skill. ³⁰In the past God overlooked such ignorance, but now he commands all people everywhere to repent. ³¹For he has set a day when he will judge the world with justice by the man he has appointed. He has given proof of this to all men by raising him from the dead."

³²When they heard about the resurrection of the dead, some of them sneered, but others said, "We want to hear you again on this subject." ³³At that, Paul left the Council. ³⁴A few men became followers of Paul and believed. Among them was Dionysius, a member of the Areopagus, also a woman named Damaris, and a number of others.

...about today's session

1. What are some cultural changes that have occurred since 1950?

2. What extremes does Rick Warren say different churches go to in relation to the culture?

Identifying with the Story

In horseshoe groups of 6–8, explore questions as time allows.

1. When you were in school, who were you most likely to get into an argument with?

   ☐ my brother or sister   ☐ kids of the opposite sex
   ☐ my father   ☐ my friends
   ☐ my mother   ☐ nobody—I never argued.
   ☐ other:_____

2. Where was the place you and your friends most frequently gathered to talk things over?

   ☐ a local soda fountain or drive-in
   ☐ a school playground
   ☐ the swimming pool
   ☐ a neighborhood park
   ☐ a friend's house
   ☐ We just talked on the phone.

3. In the town or city you grew up in, what would you say were the "gods" of the town?

   ☐ Sports—They worshiped the local _____ team.
   ☐ Money—They would do anything for a buck.
   ☐ Sex—It was a regular Peyton Place.
   ☐ The Status Quo—Anyone challenging it was exiled.
   ☐ The Perfect Lawn—Anyone stepping on one had violated "Holy Ground."
   ☐ other: _____

today's session

What is God teaching you from this story?

1. What "greatly distressed" Paul when he was in Athens?

2. What are some examples of things Christians find shocking today?

11

101

3. How did Paul use affirmation in his ministry?

4. Why is affirmation important in helping people to change?

5. When in Athens, why did Paul refer to the sayings of Greek poets instead of quoting Old Testament prophecy?

6. Paul knew that apart from _____, this new faith would have no reason for existence and would have nothing to say to anyone.

Learning from the Story

**⊍ In
horseshoe
groups of 6–8,
choose an
answer and
explain why
you chose
what you did.**

1. What surprises you the most in this story?
   - ☐ That a sophisticated traveler like Paul would be shocked by the idols of Athens.
   - ☐ That the idol-worshiping Greeks seemed to listen to Paul better than the Jews did.
   - ☐ That Paul knew and quoted Greek poets.
   - ☐ That people then scoffed at the idea of a resurrection.
   - ☐ That Paul made converts even in a sophisticated audience such as this.
   - ☐ other:_____

2. What do you think convinced these Athenians to give Paul a chance to speak in the Areopagus?
   - ☐ his eloquence
   - ☐ the power and influence of the Holy Spirit
   - ☐ their curiosity
   - ☐ their hunger for the answers Paul was giving them
   - ☐ other:_____

3. What do you think was the most effective thing Paul did in Athens?

☐ He affirmed their religious inclinations.
☐ He referred to the poets and thinkers of Greece.
☐ He showed the fallacy of worshiping gods made by hands.
☐ He boldly proclaimed the resurrection to those who were skeptical about it.
☐ other:_____

life change lessons

How can you apply this session to your life?

Write your answers here.

1. What are some examples of cultures to which we need to reach out?

2. With what expressions of youth culture are we encouraged to familiarize ourselves?

Caring Time

15-20 minutes

CARING TIME

↻ **Remain in horseshoe groups of 6–8.**

During this time, have everyone in the group share prayer requests and pray for one another. Begin by having each member answer the question:

*"If you had Paul before you right now,
what would be the biggest question in relation to God
that you would want him to address?"*

Pray for guidance on these questions. In addition, pray for the concerns on the Prayer/Praise Report.

11

Reference Notes

Use these notes to gain further understanding
of the text as you study on your own.

**ACTS
17:17**

Paul preached not only in the synagogue at Athens, but also in their marketplace where, three centuries before, Socrates likewise debated with anyone who would listen.

**ACTS
17:18**

Epicurean and Stoic philosophers. Epicurus maintained that a tranquil life free from pain, passions, and fears was the highest good for humanity. This could be achieved only by detaching oneself from indulgence and the cares of the world. The Epicureans were practical atheists in that they believed the gods had no interest in humanity and were unknowable. The Stoics had a pantheistic idea of god as the World-Soul. People were a spark of the divine; upon death one's immortal soul would be absorbed into the divine spirit. The ideal life was one of virtue that refused to give in before the pressures of circumstances and of human passions.

this babbler. Literally, "seed-picker." A derisive term stemming from the actions of a bird that picks up seeds wherever it can find them. To the philosophers, Paul seemed like someone who picked up scraps of ideas here and there and then had the audacity to try to teach others.

foreign gods ... Jesus and the resurrection. Since the Greek word for Jesus sounds something like the Greek name for the goddess of health, and since the Greek word for salvation is also used to speak of physical healing, his listeners thought Paul was talking about two new gods—Health and Resurrection.

**ACTS
17:19**

Areopagus. Athens was a free city within the Roman Empire so the Areopagus had legal and judicial authority over what went on in the city. It does not appear that Paul himself is on trial (as though he was accused of breaking any laws) as much as his message itself is being evaluated as to its credibility and worth.

**ACTS
17:21**

Luke's rather sarcastic observation about the nature of the Athenian in general is an echo of what the Greek orator Demosthenes had said 400 years earlier: "You are the best people at being deceived by something new that is said."

**ACTS
17:23**

TO AN UNKNOWN GOD. Other writers of the time speak of statues and altars in Athens raised to gods "both known and unknown." The implicit admission of ignorance about God provided Paul with a point of entry for sharing the gospel.

ACTS **17:24**	Paul asserts that God is not the uninterested or distant god of Greek philosophy. ***does not live in temples.*** Euripides, a Greek philosopher, recognized this when he wrote, "What house built by craftsman could enclose the ... divine within enfolding walls?"
ACTS **17:25**	***he is not served by human hands.*** With this, the philosopher would also agree. Plato had written, "What advantage accrues to the gods from what they get from us?"
ACTS **17:26**	The Athenians had a tradition that they were different from other people in that they had sprung up from the soil of Athens itself (they were unique among other Greeks in that they had no tradition of how their ancestors migrated into the area). Paul's point is that they, like all people, derive from God's creation of humanity.
ACTS **17:27**	Challenging the Epicurean assumption that God was unknowable, Paul says that God is knowable by those who seek after Him. While the Stoics would agree with the nearness of God, the ideas of His separateness from creation and that one could know God personally would challenge them.
ACTS **17:28**	Paul supports his points by quoting two Greek authors, Epimenides and Aratus. Both are from works about Zeus, and both were interpreted by the Stoics to refer to the *Logos*, the supreme source of reason and pride in the universe. These quotes do not imply Paul is equating Zeus with God, but it does indicate he recognized that God revealed truth about Himself even through other religions and philosophies.
ACTS **17:30**	***God overlooked such ignorance.*** This reflects the Old Testament notion that sins committed in ignorance are less culpable than those done in defiance.
ACTS **17:32–34**	The converts included Dionysius, a member of the Athenian council. Nothing more is said in the New Testament about Athens, so it is unlikely that these believers established a church at the time.

11

notes

When Faith is "Bad for Business"

Prepare for the Session

	READINGS	REFLECTIVE QUESTIONS
Monday	Acts 19:23-27	How have your business dealings reflected your beliefs? Is there anything that needs to change?
Tuesday	Acts 19:28-34	In what difficult situation do you need to stand up for Christ? What obstacles are in your way?
Wednesday	Acts 19:35-41	Does anyone have a grievance against you? How can you reconcile with this person?
Thursday	Acts 23:6-11	What are you needing courage to do at this moment in your life? Can you trust God to give you this courage?
Friday	Acts 24:10-16	Is your conscience clear? If not, what do you need to do to make it clear? Make a confession? Appeal to God's grace?
Saturday	Acts 26:22-29	Are you trying to free people of their "chains" or put them in the same "chains" that shackle you?
Sunday	Acts 27:27-29	What is anchoring your life right now? Are your "anchors" holding when you go through "storms"?

12

BIBLE STUDY
- to consider how the gospel affected business interests in Ephesus
- to consider the relationship of faith to business practices
- to appreciate what it means to make Christ Lord of all of our life

LIFE CHANGE
- to gather a support group of other Christians in a similar line of work to help each other deal with ethical dilemmas
- to affirm one person in authority above us, in his sensitivity to the need for ethical business practices
- to pray daily for our business and ask for God's guidance on how to work ethically and effectively at the same time

Icebreaker

10-15 minutes

**GATHERING
THE PEOPLE
◡ Form
horseshoe
groups of 6–8.**

What a Riot! Go around the group on question 1 and have everyone answer. Then go around again on question 2.

1. Which of the following situations would most likely raise a riot in your household? (For those living alone, which would have raised a riot in your family of origin?)

   ☐ the television goes on the fritz
   ☐ the mother takes a full-time job
   ☐ one of the kids is asked to do a job they don't normally do
   ☐ dinner isn't ready on time
   ☐ the men have to iron their own clothes
   ☐ the telephone is out of order
   ☐ one bathroom is out of order and the other held hostage by a teenager
   ☐ a parent tries to clean up a teenager's room

2. Finish this sentence: "The way I personally would be most likely to cause a riot would be by ..."

- ☐ stereotyping women while at a NOW convention.
- ☐ wearing my swimsuit in public.
- ☐ rooting for the other team while at the home team's park.
- ☐ being loud and obnoxious at a demonstration for my favorite cause.
- ☐ going too slow in the fast lane.
- ☐ making a scene at a nice restaurant over food that wasn't what I ordered.
- ☐ other: _____

Information to Remember: Finish the following sentences as you look around at the people here today.

1. The person in the group who has the biggest smile today is:

2. The person in the group who looks like he or she could use a hug is:

Bible Study
30-45 minutes

The Scripture for this week:

LEARNING
FROM THE
BIBLE

ACTS
19:23–41

²³*About that time there arose a great disturbance about the Way.* ²⁴*A silversmith named Demetrius, who made silver shrines of Artemis, brought in no little business for the craftsmen.* ²⁵*He called them together, along with the workmen in related trades, and said: "Men, you know we receive a good income from this business.* ²⁶*And you see and hear how this fellow Paul has convinced and led astray large numbers of people here in Ephesus and in practically the whole province of Asia. He says that man-made gods are no gods at all.* ²⁷*There is danger not only that our trade will lose its good name, but also that the temple of the great goddess Artemis will be discredited, and the goddess herself, who is worshiped throughout the province of Asia and the world, will be robbed of her divine majesty."*

12

[28]When they heard this, they were furious and began shouting: "Great is Artemis of the Ephesians!" [29]Soon the whole city was in an uproar. The people seized Gaius and Aristarchus, Paul's traveling companions from Macedonia, and rushed as one man into the theater. [30]Paul wanted to appear before the crowd, but the disciples would not let him. [31]Even some of the officials of the province, friends of Paul, sent him a message begging him not to venture into the theater.

[32]The assembly was in confusion: Some were shouting one thing, some another. Most of the people did not even know why they were there. [33]The Jews pushed Alexander to the front, and some of the crowd shouted instructions to him. He motioned for silence in order to make a defense before the people. [34]But when they realized he was a Jew, they all shouted in unison for about two hours: "Great is Artemis of the Ephesians!"

[35]The city clerk quieted the crowd and said: "Men of Ephesus, doesn't all the world know that the city of Ephesus is the guardian of the temple of the great Artemis and of her image, which fell from heaven? [36]Therefore, since these facts are undeniable, you ought to be quiet and not do anything rash. [37]You have brought these men here, though they have neither robbed temples nor blasphemed our goddess. [38]If, then, Demetrius and his fellow craftsmen have a grievance against anybody, the courts are open and there are proconsuls. They can press charges. [39]If there is anything further you want to bring up, it must be settled in a legal assembly. [40]As it is, we are in danger of being charged with rioting because of today's events. In that case we would not be able to account for this commotion, since there is no reason for it." [41]After he had said this, he dismissed the assembly.

...about today's session

1. What securities trader was known for his assertion "greed is good"? What happened to him?

2. What three things took ethics prisoner-of-war in the 1990s?

Identifying with the Story

In horseshoe groups of 6–8, explore questions as time allows.

1. In this story, I identify most with:

   ☐ Demetrius—because I have to deal with do-gooders who hurt my business.
   ☐ the craftsmen—because I'm easily aroused to anger.
   ☐ Gaius and Aristarchus—generally I'm the "innocent bystander" who gets dragged in.
   ☐ the friendly officials of the province—I always have to get someone out of hot water.
   ☐ the city clerk—I'm generally one who does things by orderly process.
   ☐ Paul—I cause a lot of trouble just telling it like it is.

2. When have you been in a place where, like some in this crowd, you didn't even know why you were there?

   ☐ in a church worship service
   ☐ at a family reunion or gathering
   ☐ in a church business or committee meeting
   ☐ at work
   ☐ at a party or social function
   ☐ when I went to college
   ☐ This describes most of my life!
   ☐ other: _____

3. In moments of crisis, who has supplied the "voice of reason" in your life, like the city clerk supplied in Ephesus?

   ☐ one of my parents   ☐ my spouse
   ☐ myself   ☐ a friend
   ☐ nobody—and I need that!
   ☐ nobody—and I'm glad—I hate it when people are so reasonable!

today's session

What is God teaching you from this story?

1. What saying from the movie *Jerry Maguire* typifies our culture's obsession with money?

12

2. How long did Paul's mission in Ephesus last?

3. What goddess was at the center of the silversmith trade in Ephesus?

4. What did the craftsmen of Ephesus do to avoid listening to any voice of reason?

5. What problems arise when we make money our security?

6. What did Jesus say we should seek first?

Learning from the Story

In horseshoe groups of 6–8, choose an answer and explain why you chose what you did.

1. Had you been called upon to moderate the dispute between Paul and the "local silversmith's union," what might you have said?

2. If you were to put a percentage on the degree Demetrius was concerned with his income, and the degree he was concerned about Artemis being robbed of her "divine majesty," what percentage would you assign to both?

- ☐ 10% income; 90% "divine majesty"
- ☐ 25% income; 75% "divine majesty"
- ☐ 50% income; 50% "divine majesty"
- ☐ 75% income; 25% "divine majesty"
- ☐ 90% income; 10% "divine majesty"

3. How would you finish this sentence: "When Christian faith implies things that seem bad for business, a Christian should ..."

life change lessons

How can you apply this session to your life?

Write your answers here.

1. What electronics firm is pointed to as an example of a successful, ethical business?

2. What biblical characters remind us of how God provides for those who confront powerful forces and stand their ground?

Caring Time

15-20 minutes

CARING TIME

◊ Remain in horseshoe groups of 6–8.

Come together now for a time of sharing and prayer. Begin by having each person in the group finish the statement:

"The area of my life that seems really chaotic right now is ..."

Pray for these areas of concern, and for the concerns listed on the Prayer/Praise Report.

Pray specifically for God to guide you to someone to invite for next week to fill the empty chair.

12

Reference Notes

Use these notes to gain further understanding
of the text as you study on your own.

**ACTS
19:24**

A silversmith. The silversmith trade made a great deal of money through
the manufacture and sale of models of the goddess Artemis. Artemis was
a goddess who combined belief in the Roman virgin goddess Diana with
an Asian fertility goddess. The center for her worship was in Ephesus
where an image of her (actually a meteorite) was placed in a temple that
was one of the seven wonders of the ancient world. In the spring, there
was a festival in her honor marked by crowds flocking to Ephesus for a
celebration that included orgies and general carousing.

**ACTS
19:29**

Gaius and Aristarchus. These men were among those who accompanied
Paul when he left Ephesus (20:4). Unable to find Paul, the crowd grabbed
two of his associates to accuse.

The theater. While this was the usual place for public meetings, it would
have been especially appropriate in this case since the great temple of
Artemis could be clearly seen from it.

**ACTS
19:30–31**

Both the Christians and some of the officials (these were the *asiarchs*, the
chief citizens out of whose ranks the officials of the Roman cult of emperor
worship were elected for one-year terms of office) urged Paul not to go into
the theater for fear of his safety. The protection of the *asiarchs* is another
example of official Roman protection and tolerance of Paul (18:14-17).

**ACTS
19:33–34**

The Jews, perhaps to disassociate themselves from the charges being made
against Paul, tried to have one of their number (Alexander) make a statement. However, since the Jews were well known to be against idolatry as
well, he was shouted down by the crowd before he could even speak.

**ACTS
19:35**

The city clerk. This was the highest-ranking official in the city, accountable to the Roman provincial government for what happened in Ephesus.
Not wanting to be charged with rioting, which could lead to penalties for
the city, he worked to quiet down the crowd and dismiss them.

her image, which fell from heaven. See note above on 19:24.

**ACTS
19:37**

robbed temples. Wealthy people would deposit treasures at temples for
safekeeping in light of the sacred nature of the place.

**ACTS
19:38**

proconsuls. Provinces that did not require troops to maintain order were
administered by the Roman Senate through a proconsul. Typically, there
was only one at a time over a given area.

legal assembly. The people could gather for meetings to discuss issues that concerned them, but they were to be held at set times and with a set procedure. Such an irregular, chaotic meeting as this one could lead to Roman suppression of their right to assemble. The crowd, mindful of the implied warning, dispersed.

notes

An Irrepressible Boldness

Prepare for the Session

	READINGS	REFLECTIVE QUESTIONS
Monday	Acts 28:1-6	From what "vipers" has God protected you? Have you given Him the glory for this?
Tuesday	Acts 28:15-16	Who has gone out of their way for you? Have you thanked God for them?
Wednesday	Acts 28:17-20	How has your hope in Christ taken you through trials? Has that hope remained strong?
Thursday	Acts 28:21-23	How persistent are you in sharing your faith in Christ?
Friday	Acts 28:24-26	What have you heard from teachers of the faith that you still don't understand? Who could help you to a clearer understanding?
Saturday	Acts 28:27-28	To what has your heart become calloused? People in need? The call of God? Pray for God to touch your heart anew.
Sunday	Acts 28:30-31	What would it mean for you to "boldly and without hindrance" live out your faith in Christ?

13

BIBLE STUDY
- to see how Paul's boldness in witnessing was not suppressed by his imprisonment
- to consider what it means to boldly witness for Christ today
- to encourage Christians to witness, even when in tough circumstances

LIFE CHANGE
- to write out a brief statement of what Christ has done for us
- to make a list of those to whom God is leading us
- to share our story with the people on our list, after praying for them

Icebreaker

10-15 minutes

**GATHERING
THE PEOPLE
⊍ Form
horseshoe
groups of 6–8.**

Group Warrants. Normally groups try to build an atmosphere of supportiveness, but this time we are asking you to turn "state's evidence" against your other group members! Decide which of your group members ought to be served with each of the following warrants. Write the name of one group member next to each category. Then go around the group, one person at a time, and have the others serve their warrants.

_____ for Grand Theft—You stole our hearts with your warmth.

_____ for Assault—You fought against the pretenses we try to use to hide the truth from ourselves and others.

_____ for Insurrection—You stood up against the values of this world.

_____ for Reckless Driving—You steered us through some dangerous areas with little thought of playing it safe.

_____ for Aiding and Abetting—You nurtured the spiritual growth of the group.

_____ for Creating a Disturbance—Your humor and crazy ways kept things from getting too predictable.

_____ for Arson—You set the group on fire with the Spirit.

Information to Remember: Finish the following sentences as you look around at the people here today.

1. A person in the group I would like to hear from more today is:

2. A person whom God may be leading me to say something special to today is:

Bible Study

30-45 minutes

The Scripture for this week:

LEARNING
FROM THE
BIBLE

ACTS
28:16–31

[16]When we got to Rome, Paul was allowed to live by himself, with a soldier to guard him.

[17]Three days later he called together the leaders of the Jews. When they had assembled, Paul said to them: "My brothers, although I have done nothing against our people or against the customs of our ancestors, I was arrested in Jerusalem and handed over to the Romans. [18]They examined me and wanted to release me, because I was not guilty of any crime deserving death. [19]But when the Jews objected, I was compelled to appeal to Caesar—not that I had any charge to bring against my own people. [20]For this reason I have asked to see you and talk with you. It is because of the hope of Israel that I am bound with this chain."

[21]They replied, "We have not received any letters from Judea concerning you, and none of the brothers who have come from there has reported or said anything bad about you. [22]But we want to hear what your views are, for we know that people everywhere are talking against this sect."

[23]They arranged to meet Paul on a certain day, and came in even larger numbers to the place where he was staying. From morning till evening he explained and declared to them the kingdom of God and tried to convince them about Jesus from the Law of Moses and from the Prophets. [24]Some were convinced by what he said, but others would not believe. [25]They disagreed among themselves and began to leave after Paul had made this final statement: "The Holy Spirit spoke the truth to your forefathers when he said through Isaiah the prophet:

13

26" 'Go to this people and say,
   "You will be ever hearing but never understanding;
   you will be ever seeing but never perceiving."
27For this people's heart has become calloused;
   they hardly hear with their ears,
   and they have closed their eyes.
Otherwise they might see with their eyes,
   hear with their ears,
   understand with their hearts
and turn, and I would heal them.'

28"Therefore I want you to know that God's salvation has been sent to the Gentiles, and they will listen!"

30For two whole years Paul stayed there in his own rented house and welcomed all who came to see him. 31Boldly and without hindrance he preached the kingdom of God and taught about the Lord Jesus Christ.

...about today's session

1. What were some of the things that happened in the life of Paul between last week's study and this week's?

2. Why was Paul brought to Rome?

Identifying with the Story

U In
horseshoe
groups of 6–8,
explore
questions as
time allows.

1. Finish this sentence in one of the following ways, or pick your own: "The most trouble I have been in with the law was when ..."

☐ I went joyriding as an adolescent.
☐ I shoplifted as a child or adolescent.
☐ well, there was that traffic ticket ...
☐ my taxes were audited.
☐ I tore off that mattress tag that says, "Do not remove under penalty of law."
☐ "I would tell you ... but then I would have to kill you!"
☐ other: _____

2. For whom in your life does it seem true that when you speak, they "hardly hear with their ears" (v. 27)?

☐ my children   ☐ my parents   ☐ the government
☐ my spouse   ☐ my boss   ☐ other:_____

3. If you were called before a group of people to defend how you have lived your life, as Paul was, what would you say?

What is God teaching you from this story?

today's session

1. In Acts 4:13, why was the Sanhedrin amazed at the boldness of Peter and John?

2. What were some of the letters Paul probably wrote while imprisoned in Rome?

3. What are two perspectives on the end result of Paul's imprisonment at Rome?

4. What did proclaiming Christ with boldness mean for Paul?

    a. _____

    b. _____

    c. _____

    d. _____

    e. _____

5. Why had friends warned Paul not to go to Jerusalem? Why did he go anyway?

13

Learning from the Story

☾ In horseshoe groups of 6–8, choose an answer and explain why you chose what you did.

1. How would you describe Paul as you see him in this last story of Acts? (Check as many characteristics as apply.)

   ☐ defensive   ☐ bold
   ☐ optimistic   ☐ bitter
   ☐ zealous   ☐ irrepressible
   ☐ frustrated   ☐ weary
   ☐ stubborn   ☐ other:_____
   ☐ confident

2. What would you say seems to be Paul's main concern in this passage?

   ☐ justifying his life
   ☐ spreading the gospel
   ☐ gaining his freedom
   ☐ denouncing his enemies
   ☐ other: _____

3. The most influential factor in Paul being able to preach the gospel boldly while under arrest was:

   ☐ Paul's irrepressible personality
   ☐ the power of the Holy Spirit
   ☐ his knowledge that God was with him
   ☐ the companionship of believers who supported him
   ☐ other: _____

life change lessons

How can you apply this session to your life?

Write your answers here.

1. What is the reason presented by the leader that many people today don't share their faith? Do you agree with this analysis?

2. "Boldness does not have to mean being _____."

122

Caring Time

15-20 minutes

CARING TIME

⊍ **Remain in horseshoe groups of 6–8.**

Pray for the concerns listed on the Prayer/Praise Report, then continue with the evaluation and covenant.

1. Take some time to evaluate the life of your group by using the statements below. Read the first sentence out loud and ask everyone to explain where they would put a dot between the two extremes. When you are finished, go back and give your group an overall grade in the categories of Group Building, Bible Study, and Mission.

GROUP BUILDING

On celebrating life and having fun together, we were more like a ...
wet blanket · hot tub

On becoming a caring community, we were more like a ...
prickly porcupine · cuddly teddy bear

BIBLE STUDY

On sharing our spiritual stories, we were more like a ...
shallow pond · spring-fed lake

On digging into Scripture, we were more like a ...
slow-moving snail · voracious anteater

MISSION

On inviting new people into our group, we were more like a ...
barbed-wire fence · wide-open door

On stretching our vision for mission, we were more like an ...
ostrich · eagle

13

2. What are some specific areas in which you have grown in this course?

- [ ] being more open to the Holy Spirit's guidance
- [ ] finding new ways to minister to other's needs
- [ ] handling conflict situations in the church with love and wisdom
- [ ] sharing faith and fellowship with other cultures
- [ ] understanding the power of prayer
- [ ] slowing down and letting the Holy Spirit guide me
- [ ] following ethical business practices
- [ ] other:_____

A covenant is a promise made to another in the presence of God. Its purpose is to indicate your intention to make yourselves available to one another for the fulfillment of the purposes you share in common. If your group is going to continue, in a spirit of prayer work your way through the following sentences, trying to reach an agreement on each statement pertaining to your ongoing life together. Write out your covenant like a contract, stating your purpose, goals, and the ground rules for your group.

1. The purpose of our group will be:

2. Our goals will be:

3. We will meet on _____ (day of week).

4. We will meet for _____weeks, after which we will decide if we wish to continue as a group.

5. We will meet from _____ to _____ and we will strive to start on time and end on time.

6. We will meet at _____ (place) or we will rotate from house to house.

7. We will agree to the following ground rules for our group (check):

☐ **PRIORITY:** While you are in this course of study, you give the group meetings priority.

☐ **PARTICIPATION:** Everyone is encouraged to participate and no one dominates.

☐ **RESPECT:** Everyone has the right to his or her own opinion, and all questions are encouraged and respected.

☐ **CONFIDENTIALITY:** Anything said in the meeting is never repeated outside the meeting.

☐ **LIFE CHANGE:** We will regularly assess our own life change goals and encourage one another in our pursuit of Christlikeness.

☐ **EMPTY CHAIR:** The group stays open to reaching new people at every meeting.

☐ **CARE and SUPPORT:** Permission is given to call upon each other at any time especially in times of crisis. The group will provide care for every member.

☐ **ACCOUNTABILITY:** We agree to let the members of the group hold us accountable to the commitments which each of us make in whatever loving ways we decide upon.

☐ **MISSION:** We will do everything in our power to start a new group.

☐ **MINISTRY:** The group will encourage one another to volunteer and serve in a ministry, and to support missions by giving financially and/or personally serving.

13

Reference Notes

Use these notes to gain further understanding
of the text as you study on your own.

**ACTS
28:16**

Paul was allowed to live by himself. Paul was not kept in a prison, but kept under guard in a type of house arrest while he awaited trial. He may have been able to work as a leather-worker during this time, or gifts from the churches that cared for him may have provided for his needs (Phil. 4:14-18).

**ACTS
28:17–22**

As soon as possible, Paul called together the leaders of the synagogues in Rome (at least 13 are known to have existed). He held this meeting in order to explain his situation to them first-hand so they might not be influenced more by rumors than personal information.

**ACTS
28:19**

my own people. Notice also "my brothers" and "our ancestors" (v. 17). Once again, Luke presents Paul as a faithful Jew; his commitment to Jesus as the Messiah is to be seen as a natural outgrowth of his trust in the Old Testament Scriptures and his loyalty to God (v. 20; 23:6; 24:15; 26:22-23). His appeal to Caesar is not to be construed as trying to bring any problems to the Jews either in Rome or Jerusalem.

**ACTS
28:22**

people everywhere are talking about this sect. A church had been established among the Jewish community in Rome for at least 20 years and perhaps as far back as Pentecost nearly 30 years earlier (2:10). Paul's letter to Rome, written about three years before his arrival, deals extensively with conflicts arising between Jewish and Gentile elements in the church there. Thus, these Jewish leaders certainly knew something of Christianity, but they may have desired to finally get some answers to questions that had never been clearly explained to them.

**ACTS
28:23**

Examples of how Paul argued for the gospel from the Old Testament Scriptures are given in 13:16-41; 22:3–21 and 26:4-27.

the kingdom of God. Throughout the Gospels, the message of Jesus is known as the message of the kingdom of God (Mark 1:15). This phrase serves as summary of what the entire gospel is about—it announces the present and coming reign of God in human affairs and calls people to affirm their loyalty to Jesus as God's appointed King.

**ACTS
28:25–27**

Paul accounts for the unbelief of many through the words of the prophet Isaiah in Isaiah 6:9–10 (see also Mark 4:12). In its context, this passage spoke of the fact that although God sent Isaiah to call Israel to repent, the net effect of his preaching would be that people would become even more hardened against God. Verse 27 is full of a sad irony; it is as if the people deliberately block their ears and shut their eyes to God as though the last thing they want is to turn to God and be forgiven. By quoting this passage, Paul is calling on his Jewish hearers not to follow in the footsteps of their forefathers who rejected Isaiah and his message.

Luke concludes Acts with the picture of Paul continuing his missionary activities and preaching to all who would listen.

his own rented house. See note on 28:16.

In this last statement in Acts, the emphasis in the Greek sentence falls on the boldness and freedom with which Paul preached the gospel. During this period of house arrest, Paul wrote the letter of Philippians and probably the letters of Ephesians, Colossians, and Philemon as well. Philippians 1:12-13 gives an insight to his situation during this time as he carried on an extensive ministry to the soldiers assigned to guard him, undoubtedly resulting in the conversion of a number of them. While some believe that at the end of these two years Paul was executed, other scholars contend that Paul was released and enjoyed freedom for another two years, during which he traveled once again to Crete, Asia, and Macedonia. It was during this time that it is believed he wrote the letters of 1 Timothy and Titus. According to this second perspective, at some point after this, he was again arrested and imprisoned at Rome, but this time things were far more sinister. The Emperor Nero, widely suspected of having started the great fire of Rome in A.D. 64, needed to shift the blame off of himself onto someone else and Christians were chosen as the culprits. This resulted in an outburst of cruel persecution against the church during which it is believed both Paul and Peter were executed by Roman authorities.

13

**PASS THIS DIRECTORY AROUND AND
HAVE YOUR GROUP MEMBERS FILL IN
THEIR NAMES AND PHONE NUMBERS.**

Group
Directory

NAME

PHONE

_____   _____

_____   _____

_____   _____

_____   _____

_____   _____

_____   _____

_____   _____

_____   _____

_____   _____

_____   _____

_____   _____

_____   _____

_____   _____

_____   _____